Human–Computer Interaction Series

T0180850

Human-Computer Interaction is a multidisciplinary field focused on human aspects of the development of computer technology. As computer-based technology becomes increasingly pervasive - not just in developed countries, but worldwide - the need to take a human- centered approach in the design and development of this technology becomes ever more important. For roughly 30 years now, researchers and practitioners in computational and behavioral sciences have worked to identify theory and practice that influences the direction of these technologies, and this diverse work makes up the field of human–computer interaction. Broadly speaking it includes the study of what technology might be able to do for people and how people might interact with the technology. In this series we present work which advances the science and technology of developing systems which are both effective and satisfying for people in a wide variety of contexts. The human–computer interaction series will focus on theoretical perspectives (such as formal approaches drawn from a variety of behavioral sciences), practical approaches (such as the techniques for effectively integrating user needs in system development), and social issues (such as the determinants of utility, usability and acceptability).

For further volumes:
http://www.springer.com/series/6033

Luciana Cardoso de Castro Salgado
Carla Faria Leitão • Clarisse Sieckenius de Souza

A Journey Through Cultures

Metaphors for Guiding the Design of Cross-Cultural Interactive Systems

 Springer

Luciana Cardoso de Castro Salgado
Department of Informatics
Semiotic Engineering Research Group
PUC-Rio
Rio de Janeiro, Brazil

Carla Faria Leitão
Department of Informatics
Semiotic Engineering Research Group
PUC-Rio
Rio de Janeiro, Brazil

Clarisse Sieckenius de Souza
Department of Informatics
Semiotic Engineering Research Group
PUC-Rio
Rio de Janeiro, Brazil

ISSN 1571-5035
ISBN 978-1-4471-6063-2   ISBN 978-1-4471-4114-3 (eBook)
DOI 10.1007/978-1-4471-4114-3
Springer London Heidelberg New York Dordrecht

Preface

This book has been written thanks to various kinds of collaboration among a number of people. The first one is the collaboration among the authors themselves. Luciana Salgado and Clarisse de Souza started working together in 2005, when Luciana began her M.Sc. program under Clarisse's supervision. Carla Leitão had been working with Clarisse since 2002 and, when Luciana decided to continue her graduate studies as a Ph.D. candidate, in 2007, Carla and Clarisse supervised her research together. Carla, Clarisse and Luciana then formed a very special interdisciplinary *trio* that already foreshadowed the path that would eventually lead to this book. Carla is a psychologist, with a Ph.D. in Psychology and Social Construction of Subjectivity. Clarisse is a translator and linguist, with a Ph.D. in Computational Linguistics. Luciana has a degree in Information Systems and a Ph.D. in Informatics and Computing, specializing in HCI. The three of them are senior members of the *Semiotic Engineering Research Group* (SERG) of the Department of Informatics at the Pontifical Catholic University of Rio de Janeiro (PUC-Rio).

SERG is the home of Semiotic Engineering, a semiotic theory of HCI that has been gaining increased interest in recent years. This is the third book internationally published by SERG authors about Semiotic Engineering. The first, with a comprehensive introduction to the theory by Clarisse de Souza, was published in 2005 (*The Semiotic Engineering of Human-Computer Interaction*, MIT Press). The second, by Clarisse de Souza and Carla Leitão, focused specifically on Semiotic Engineering methodology and was published in 2009 (*Semiotic Engineering Methods for Scientific Research in HCI*, Morgan & Claypool). The present book presents the results of Luciana Salgado's Ph.D. thesis and constitutes a major leap in the theoretical basis of Semiotic Engineering. The inclusion of the cultural dimension in the scope of our studies has given us a whole new platform to think not only about the design of cross-cultural computer systems, but also about HCI itself.

We are deeply thankful to Karin Breitman, Assistant Professor in our department at PUC-Rio and Director of Publications for the Brazilian Computer Society. She is the one who encouraged us to publish Luciana's thesis as a book. She put us in contact with Beverley Ford, at Springer, whom we would also like to thank for leading this project ahead with great professionalism, always encouraging and helping us carry it through. The end result owes much to the excellent editorial guidance we had from Ben Bishop and his team while preparing this volume.

We extend our gratitude to our colleagues at SERG, past and present, whose stimulating questions and unconditional support have brought us this far. We are also deeply grateful to all the volunteers who participated in so many experiments throughout the years of research behind this book.

Additionally, we must thank our colleagues, students and staff members in the Department of Informatics at PUC-Rio for providing us the right atmosphere and the means to do our work. We are especially indebted to the sponsors of various sub-projects that contributed to the results reported in this book: the National Council for Scientific and Technological Development (CNPq) and the Carlos Chagas Filho Research Foundation of the State of Rio de Janeiro (FAPERJ).

Writing this book has been a major summer project for the three of us. During this time our families and friends have gotten much less of our attention than they deserve. They have loved and supported us all the same. Our dear families have been the source of our strength and inspiration to conclude this book, which we dedicate to them with all our love.

Rio de Janeiro   Luciana Cardoso de Castro Salgado
                                                            Carla Faria Leitão
                                              Clarisse Sieckenius de Souza

Contents

1 Introduction.. 1
   1.1 On Design and HCI Design... 2
   1.2 Semiotic Engineering.. 4
   1.3 Towards the Semiotic Engineering of Cross-Cultural Systems........ 9
   1.4 On the Content and Structure of This Book................................... 15
   References.. 16

2 Semiotic Engineering and Culture 19
   2.1 An Overview of Semiotic Engineering Theory 20
   2.2 Definitions for Culture and Their Influence
        on Semiotic Engineering.. 30
   2.3 Culture-Sensitive Interaction: How Semiotic Engineering
        Frames Cross-Cultural Design 36
   References.. 40

3 Cultural Viewpoint Metaphors.. 43
   3.1 Cultural Viewpoint Metaphors as a Top Level Frame
        for Cross-Cultural HCI Design 44
       3.1.1 The Domestic Traveler Metaphor 47
       3.1.2 The Observer at a Distance Metaphor.................................. 48
       3.1.3 The Guided Tour Visitor Metaphor...................................... 52
       3.1.4 The Foreigner with Translator Metaphor 56
       3.1.5 The Foreigner Without Translator Metaphor 60
   References.. 66

4 A Case Study: Re-designing the AVIS Website 69
   4.1 Step One: Cultural Viewpoint Metaphors at Design Time 72
       4.1.1 Detailed Results 74
       4.1.2 Summarized Results.. 86
   4.2 Step Two: Cultural Viewpoint Metaphors at Evaluation Time 87
       4.2.1 Detailed Results 91
       4.2.2 Summarized Results.. 99

4.3   Final Analysis and Synthesis of Results 100
4.4   Triangulation 101
        4.4.1   Evaluating FIFA Website with CVM 102
        4.4.2   Results 106
4.5   Contrasting Findings from the Studies with AVIS
        and FIFA Websites 111
References 113

5   **Final Discussion** 115
    References 124

Index 127

List of Figures

Fig. 1.1   Localized Website   5
Fig. 1.2   International Website   6
Fig. 1.3   The general schema of metacommunication
in human-computer interaction   7
Fig. 1.4   System modules with culturally-adapted interface designs   11
Fig. 1.5   CVM for organizing intercultural metacommunication   13
Fig. 1.6   Sketch of alternative ICDL interface for Brazilian school   14

Fig. 2.1   Interlocutors involved in metacommunication in HCI   21
Fig. 2.2   The Semiotic Engineering design space   22
Fig. 2.3   Terra Culinária website (Hamburger recipe)   27
Fig. 2.4   Jamie Oliver website (coconut pancakes)   28
Fig. 2.5   Allrecipes.com website (homepage)   29
Fig. 2.6   The semiotic engineering design space
including cultural diversity   38

Fig. 3.1   Progressive cultural viewpoint metaphors   45
Fig. 3.2   Metaphors' effects while expressing design intent   46
Fig. 3.3   The domestic traveler metaphor   47
Fig. 3.4   Recipe.com website (Cheese Fondue recipe)   49
Fig. 3.5   The observer at a distance metaphor   50
Fig. 3.6   Global Gourmet website (global destinations)   51
Fig. 3.7   Global Gourmet website (destination: Austria)   52
Fig. 3.8   Global Gourmet website (chocolate pudding recipe)   53
Fig. 3.9   The guided tour visitor metaphor   53
Fig. 3.10   Culinary.net website (articles)   55
Fig. 3.11   Culinary.net website (Parfait recipe)   56
Fig. 3.12   Just Brazil website (recipes)   57
Fig. 3.13   Just Brazil website (Caldeirada de Mariscos)   58
Fig. 3.14   SoniaPortuguese.com website   59
Fig. 3.15   The foreigner with translator metaphor   59
Fig. 3.16   Brazilian recipes website   61

Fig. 3.17   Brazilian recipes website (cheese bread recipe) 62
Fig. 3.18   The foreigner without translator metaphor 62
Fig. 3.19   Online recipe guide website 63
Fig. 3.20   The amazon.com home page 64

Fig. 4.1   Research steps 70
Fig. 4.2   The structure of the task model for making a car
            reservation in the AVIS website 73
Fig. 4.3   P1.1's mockup guided by the foreigner with translator
            metaphor: 'Select a car' webpage 82
Fig. 4.4   P1.1's mockup guided by the guided tour visitor
            metaphor: 'Home page' 82
Fig. 4.5   P1.1's mockup guided by the guided tour visitor
            metaphor: 'Select a car' webpage 83
Fig. 4.6   P1.2's mockup guided by the observer at a distance
            metaphor: 'Home page' 84
Fig. 4.7   Portion of P1.2's mockup guided by the observer
            at a distance metaphor 84
Fig. 4.8   P1.2's mockup guided by the guided tour visitor
            metaphor: 'Home page' 85
Fig. 4.9   P1.2's mockup guided by the guided tour visitor
            metaphor: 'Select a car' page 85
Fig. 4.10   P1.2's homepage mockup guided by the foreigner
            with translator metaphor 86
Fig. 4.11   P1.2's handmade mockup 88
Fig. 4.12   P1.2' Balsamiq mockup 89
Fig. 4.13   Videos of click-through Balsamiq mockups 90
Fig. 4.14   Triangulation: CVM at evaluation time 102
Fig. 4.15   FIFA website in English 104
Fig. 4.16   2010 FIFA World Cup South Africa's portion
            of FIFA website 105

List of Tables

Table 3.1   The domestic traveler metaphor effects
             on metacommunication   48
Table 3.2   The observer at a distance metaphor effects
             on metacommunication   50
Table 3.3   The guided tour visitor metaphor effects
             on metacommunication   54
Table 3.4   The foreigner with translator metaphor effects
             on metacommunication   60
Table 3.5   The foreigner without translator metaphor effects
             on metacommunication   63
Table 3.6   Cultural viewpoint metaphors   65
Table 4.1   Participants' cultural background and corresponding
             targeted user   73
Table 4.2   The distribution of alternatives and scenario
             among participants   89
Table 5.1   Relations between five conceptual viewpoint metaphors 119

Chapter 1
Introduction

Abstract This chapter introduces how Semiotic Engineering, a semiotic theory of Human-Computer Interaction (HCI), connects to culture, providing the appropriate context in which we wish this book will be read. Firstly, we express our assumptions about design activities in general and about HCI design in particular. Then we briefly present our theory and some conceptual support for thinking about culture. The next step is to establish the focus of our research, the design of cross-cultural systems, which we define as systems that intentionally expose foreign material to their users. These kinds of systems are meant to engage users on journeys through cultures and designing them is a very complex task. In this book, we present Cultural Viewpoint Metaphors, a Semiotic Engineering conceptual tool to help HCI designers organize culture-sensitive interaction discourse about the journeys that users may take.

With over two billion users in 2011,[1] the World Wide Web (Web) has become a prime medium for intercultural encounters and plays a leading role in heightening both visibility and awareness of cultural diversity. Communication possibilities provided by the Web 2.0, the second generation of web applications, offer many new ways for users to interact and collaborate with each other. In applications like blogs, wikis and social-networking sites, they can create and share unlimited information and experience, not only as individuals but also as part of social groups and organizations. The Web is indeed an extension of the physical world, where an ever-increasing number of human activities *may* take place (like talking to friends, shopping, watching movies, etc.) and a growing number of others *must* take place (like e-commerce with stores that operate online only and, in a number of countries now, paying taxes, requesting government services, etc.).

One of the striking differences between the physical world and its extension online is the widely spread absence of national borders. As a rule, once users are

---

[1] Data from Internet World Stats in December 2011 (http://www.internetworldstats.com).

L.C.C. Salgado et al., *A Journey Through Cultures: Metaphors for Guiding the Design of Cross-Cultural Interactive Systems*, Human–Computer Interaction Series, DOI 10.1007/978-1-4471-4114-3_1, © Springer-Verlag London 2013

online they can navigate *anywhere*. Internet locations in one country can be accessed by users from any other country, something that economies all over the world are using as an opportunity to expand their markets and resources.

UNESCO, the United Nations Educational, Scientific and Cultural Organization, views the promotion of cultural diversity as "one of the most pressing contemporary issues", "a driving force of development, not only in respect of economic growth, but also as a means of leading a more fulfilling intellectual, emotional, moral and spiritual life" [34]. In agreement with the Information and Communication Technology (ICT) scenario described above, UNESCO underlines the role of technology in achieving its mission. The agency proclaims that "acceptance and recognition of cultural diversity – in particular through innovative use of media and ICTs – are conducive to dialogue among civilizations and cultures, respect and mutual understanding" [34].

Research and developments in twenty-first century Human-Computer Interaction (HCI) must respond to the cultural challenges brought about by globalized societies. There is an urgent need to generate a body of knowledge that will help HCI designers strike the right balance between cultural accessibility – allowing users from one culture to navigate through software produced by or to other cultures – and the preservation of cultural diversity – producing technologies that respect, express and strengthen cultural values and identity. In a word, HCI researchers and professionals are *the ones* entrusted by UNESCO to produce theories, methods, techniques and artifacts *conducive to dialogue among civilizations and cultures, respect and mutual understanding.*

This book is our share of contribution to the global challenge. We present our **Cultural Viewpoint Metaphors (CVM),** a conceptual design tool to help organize the HCI designers' communication of culture-sensitive interaction with/through computer systems [30]. As a consequence of our research, we are especially aware of the need to express and explain – to the best of our abilities – our own cultural biases and assumptions, in an effort to reach mutual understanding with our readers.

In this introduction we make brief considerations about *design* activities in general and then *HCI design* in particular. Then we show how Semiotic Engineering [8], a semiotic theory of HCI, deals with certain aspects of design more easily than other kinds of theories. Our next step is to connect Semiotic Engineering with culture, which leads us into the main topic of this book. We then elaborate a little on CVM, providing the appropriate context in which we wish this book will be read. Finally we present the structure of this book, with a short description of the contents in each chapter.

1.1   On Design and HCI Design

In his keynote address to the 2008 Annual Conference of the Design History Society, Bruno Latour [22] explored how the concept of *design* has been expanded in recent times. Today not only objects are designed, but so are city districts, social processes, and even the biological constitution of living beings. Designers are no longer those who add a veneer of form to carefully engineered objects. Their activities have penetrated the very essence of production, as well as the domains of science and technology. In Latour's words:

> [...] not only has 'natural' become a synonym of 'carefully managed', 'skillfully staged', 'artificially maintained', 'cleverly designed' [...]; but the very idea that to bring the knowledge of scientists and engineers to bear on a question is to necessarily resort to the unquestionable laws of nature, is also becoming obsolete. Bringing in scientists and engineers is quickly becoming another way of asking: 'How can it be better re-designed?' (p. 8)

The eyes of the philosopher are turned, however, to consequences of this change, which Latour characterizes as a shift from dealing with *matters of fact* to *matters of concern*. Human experience (and hence human perception and interpretation) has become so extensively *designed,* that it is now hard to establish if some objective reality (a *matter of fact*) can be distinguished from skillfully controlled states of affairs (a *matter of concern*). Underneath this change, Latour traces the characteristics in design activities that have contributed to it. Two of the discussed characteristics are particularly relevant for this book.

Firstly, design is about *meaning*. If we take a mobile phone, for example, and try to separate *matters of fact* from *matters of concern*, we are likely to fail. All the engineering that goes into building mobile phones is at the service of values and benefits that result from interpretations of the world. Thus, as is especially the case of artifacts with digital components, mobile phones are the reification of intentionally selected and carefully elaborated *signs* (representations of meanings).

Secondly, in its expansion, design has stepped into the domain of *morality*. Although we have always heard of *good* and *bad* design, as soon as it ceased to be a mere polishing of objects constructed in accordance with intrinsically *moral* natural laws, design began to deal with *social* morality. Taking this notion even further, Latour touches on political facets of design and the conflicting forces that struggle with each other in the process of elaborating human experience. Which ones make their way to the final design? How does this happen? Why are other forces subsided?

In the conclusion of his keynote address, Latour [22] challenges the audience:

> In its long history, design practice has done a marvelous job of inventing the practical skills for drawing objects, from architectural drawing, mechanic blueprints, scale models, prototyping etc. But what has always been missing from those marvelous drawings (designs in the literal sense) [is] an impression of the controversies and the many contradicting stakeholders that are born within with these. (p. 9)

In 2005, only 3 years before Latour gave his lecture for the Design History Society, Jared Spool and Eric Schaffer participated in a CHI Conference panel entitled *'The great debate: can usability scale up'* [32]. Usability, as we know, is one of the critical design mandates in HCI. Although standing in opposing sides, Spool's and Schaffer's positions shared an implicit common mismatch with Latour's views. On one side of the debate, Spool attacked User Centered Design (UCD) saying that "UCD pretends to act like an engineering discipline (formalized methods that have repeatable results independent of practitioner) but actually behaves as if it's a craft (dependent completely on skills and talents of practitioners with no repeatable results)."

(p. 1174) On the other side, Schaffer declared that the importance of usability gurus, on whose *craft* the quality of interactive digital artifacts still depends to some extent, will fade away. Soon, he says, "usability work will [...] be done in mature 'usability factories'". (p. 1174)

An impersonal and disengaged perspective on HCI design is manifest in both Spool's view of what an HCI *engineering discipline* (providing *repeatable results independent of practitioner*) should be and Schaffer's vision of *usability factories* of the future. Can the challenge launched by Latour fit into this debate? Should we be speaking of meanings, or even morality, not only of an HCI engineering discipline and usability factories? Although there are different views on what HCI is [11, 33, 37], impersonal disengaged perspectives are still widespread, possibly delaying our response to Latour. Even if we don't agree with his views, the mere thinking of why we don't is likely to be profoundly revealing of our own implicit beliefs and values.

1.2   Semiotic Engineering

As its name suggests, Semiotic Engineering [8] is a *semiotic* theory of HCI aiming to support the construction of interactive computer artifacts. Semiotics is the discipline that studies *signs*: what they are, how they are produced and used, how they are structured, classified, etc. As a consequence, *semiotic* theories of HCI are concerned with *signs* involved in human-computer interaction. Because designers and developers carefully choose and encode interface signs in order to enable users to do things with them (and thus have various kinds of experience in different contexts), interface signs put designers and developers *in communication* with users. This is the main characteristic of *semiotic* theories of HCI [1, 24], compared to cognitive theories, ergonomic theories, etc. In a word, *semiotic* theories of HCI view human-computer interaction as computer-mediated human communication.

In the early 1990s, we proposed a semiotic approach to designing interface languages [7]. In it, we defined human-computer interaction as *metacommunication*: communication *about* how, when, where and why to communicate with the system. This specific kind of metacommunication was further defined as a one-shot message, from designers to users, a complete and complex *performative* piece of communication whose meanings unfold and reveal themselves as the users interact with *it*. Over the years, Semiotic Engineering turned into a theory of HCI, with its own ontology, concepts, models and methods [8, 9].

The essence of Semiotic Engineering can be quickly illustrated with the following example. In Fig. 1.1[2] we present a sketched view of a localized website's entry page. The sketch is a snapshot, a static representation of an actual localized page on the

---

[2] The translations of Portuguese text signaled by call outs are: (1) Welcome to Site! Localized experience. Need help?; (2) Keep with the Brazilian Site; and (3) Start.

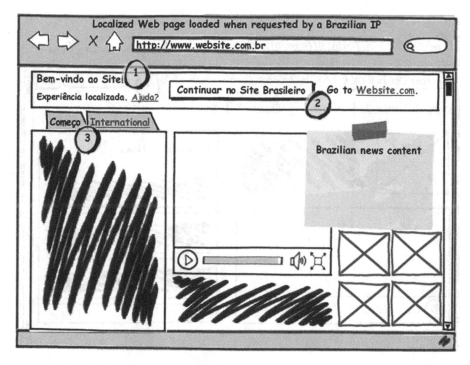

Fig. 1.1 Localized website

Web, which also contains non represented dynamic signs (that is, signs that change over time, with or without user input) such as a slide show of images and animated interface controls. It also contains special *signs about signs* (metalinguistic signs), like the Portuguese phrase "Experiência Localizada" (Localized Experience) next to call number 1. This sign refers to the meanings communicated and enabled by *all* the other interface signs on this website.

By strategically combining these three kinds of signs – static, dynamic and meta-linguistic – the designers of the website sketched in Fig. 1.1 communicate multiple individual messages to the users, which together compose the integral *one-shot message* fully programmed into the system's interface. For instance, designers are explicitly saying that they have cared to design a *localized experience*. If the users don't know what this means, they can explain it (see "Ajuda?" next to call number 1, the Portuguese equivalent of "Need Help?"). They are also saying that the users may decline their invitation for having the localized experience by clicking on one of two links: "Go to website.com" and "International". The designers' interpretation of cultural values that are important to users in Brazil are expressed mainly by their selection of local images, local news, local advertising, all in Portuguese, of course. Their choice between static and dynamic signs can call the users' attention to some parts of the interface rather than others, as well as engage them in further interactions that convey other aspects of the designers' overall message. Likewise, the presence or absence of metalinguistic signs expresses the designers' guess about which items

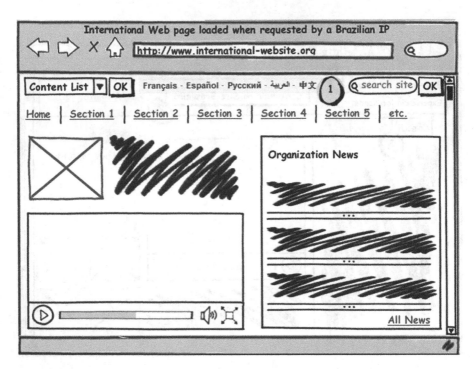

Fig. 1.2 International website

may require further explanations or more information in order to be fully understood by the users. Interestingly, the presence of metalinguistic signs also expresses the elements of the message that the *designers* really do not want the users to miss (like the meaning of a *localized experience*).

Using the same kinds of signs (static, dynamic and metalinguistic) in a different domain, the designers of the website sketched in Fig. 1.2 communicate that this other site contains material that can be read by users coming from different nations and cultures. The contents shown to all the users are the same, unlike what happens with the localized site in Fig. 1.1. However, for accessibility, the designers allow users to choose between five languages besides English (see callout 1 in Fig. 1.2): French, Spanish, Russian, Arabic or Chinese. The designers also communicate their belief that most users will be able to read *English*, since this is the language of the default entry page.

Semiotic Engineering differs from (and complements) UCD in important ways. First, communication, and not cognition, is the central phenomenon of interest in the theory. Taking Norman's Cognitive Engineering [27], for instance, as a theoretical basis for UCD, the switch from cognition to communication serves to show that *both* theories are *partial*. That is, both help us understand important aspects of HCI, but neither can account for *all* that is involved in human-computer interaction. Second, since HCI designers are in communication with users through systems interfaces, the *humans* involved in human-computer interaction are both designers

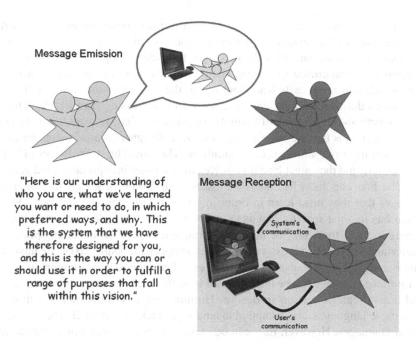

Fig. 1.3 The general schema of metacommunication in human-computer interaction

and users. Third, as the Semiotic Engineering characterization of HCI as a *one-shot metacommunication message* foreshadows, systems interfaces represent the designers at interaction time. They reply to users on the designers' behalf, they provide explanations, make invitations, etc. Note that, as is the case with the sketches in Figs. 1.1 and 1.2, in order to keep in communication with users, designers do not need to resort to anthropomorphized representations of *themselves*. Quite contrarily, the signs used in HCI *are typically not* the kinds of signs used in natural communication. Therefore, in Semiotic Engineering, HCI design is the elaboration and specification of all and only the *conversations* that designers and users can have with each other in order to achieve the goals and effects that the designed system is expected to achieve. This includes, among others, two crucially important elements that UCD theories don't account for. One is the elaboration and specification of how the designers will represent *themselves* as the *senders* of the design message (e. g. they may speak and communicate through objects, through humanoid agents, through various elements of a virtual space, etc.). The other is the choice of expressive computable sign systems, with appropriate structure and cultural references, which will enable users and designers to communicate smoothly with each other.

In Fig. 1.3 we summarize the points above and show the general schema of metacommunication in human-computer interaction. The top-level one-shot message from designers to users tells them the designers' vision (message emission). The users can only *get* the designers' message (message reception) if they interact with the system, which is in fact the designers' deputy in this specific kind of computer-mediated communication. Notice that, as is the case in human communication in general, users can react to the designers' communication even if they are not conscious of who, exactly, is communicating the messages they are getting. This means that the designers have the choice of making their presence more or less apparent to the users, which will necessarily lead them to ask themselves whose message they, as the system's designers, are *voicing* (a step towards addressing Latour's challenge).

The fourth and final aspect of Semiotic Engineering that we want to highlight in this introduction is that the interface signs used in designer-to-user[3] metacommunication must meet two simultaneous conditions. They must be strongly rooted in the users' culture and they must lend themselves to computer interpretation and generation. The first condition facilitates the users' *acquisition* of all distinct interface languages that they must learn in order to interact with computer artifacts. Every system has its *own* specific language, even if – as is the case with some human languages, too – there may be numerous similarities (and co-occurring *patterns*) in interface languages across systems that support the same tasks, or have the same brand, or run in the same platform, etc. The second condition ensures that the interface language can be implemented in software. It is easy to see that the two conditions create a tension in design. Humans are in communication through computable languages, and computable languages lack important characteristics of natural languages. However, they can be viewed as constrained *human* languages, in the sense that they are created by humans and for humans. Therefore, the *semiotic engineering* of interface languages amounts to the design and construction of designer-to-user metacommunication carried out in one or more languages that meet these two conditions. Notice that, unlike the kind of linguistic engineering that is involved in the elaboration of programming languages, the semiotic engineering of interface languages must have an elaborate model of how the language can be *used* in social contexts. It requires an elaborate *pragmatic component*, where speakers' roles, conversational contexts and structures, speech acts, cooperative dialog rules and the like are completely specified. This is what puts the process of metacommunication in effect.

This very brief presentation of Semiotic Engineering should show that this particular theory of HCI is well equipped to address the issues raised by Latour in his philosophical analysis of contemporary design [22]. In the next section of this introduction we will talk about *culture* and the HCI design of *cross-cultural systems*, which we define as systems that intentionally expose material from foreign culture(s) to their users. In particular, we illustrate how Latour's concerns mentioned above play an important role in this context and describe very briefly our CVM. The aim is to introduce why, as is our belief, Semiotic Engineering can bring relevant contributions to ongoing research about cultural aspects of human-computer interaction.

---

[3] Throughout the entire book we will often use "designer" and "user" in singular form. However, unless explicitly indicated otherwise, this is only a rhetorical choice to facilitate reading. These terms actually stand for collective objects, a team of designers and a community of users, respectively.

1.3   Towards the Semiotic Engineering of Cross-Cultural Systems

Talking about the design of cross-cultural systems requires that we adopt a consistent perspective on what constitutes *culture*. Hofstede [20] is among the most cited authors in the HCI literature dealing with culture. His definition of culture amounts to a collectivization of individual personality traits. Here is a passage where he explicitly exposes this view:

> Culture is to a human collectivity what personality is to an individual. (…) Culture could be defined as the interactive aggregate of common characteristics that influence a human group's response to its environment. Culture determines the identity of a human group in the same way as personality determines the identity of an individual. (…) Cultural traits sometimes can be measured by personality tests. (ibid., p. 21)

Hofstede's perspective is methodologically advantageous for those who are interested in predicting the behavior of cultural groups. Note the importance given to *measuring* cultural traits in the passage above. Most importantly, Hofstede follows a particular line of thought in anthropology, according to which there are generalizable cultural traits. Since our research deals with intercultural communication, with pronounced interest in the diversity of meanings that thrive in cultural groups *with* whom and *about* whom designers communicate content through computer system interfaces, cultural generalizations may lead us astray.

We have thus chosen different anthropological backing, namely Geertz's work. Known as the founder of interpretive or symbolic anthropology, Geertz has a particular view on culture, whose essence was explicitly formulated in his essay introducing the publication, in 1973, of 14 among his best known articles [14]. The passage below foreshadows our choice of his views in this book:

> The concept of culture I espouse, and whose utility the essays below attempt to demonstrate, is essentially a semiotic one. Believing, with Max Weber, that man is an animal suspended in webs of significance he himself has spun, I take culture to be those webs, and the analysis of it to be therefore not an experimental science in search of law but an interpretive one in search of meaning. (ibid., p. 5)

Because the exchange of meanings is the most fundamental process in communication, we can rely on interpretive anthropology to elicit culture-sensitive meanings that constitute a large portion of the content communicated in cross-cultural systems. For example, interpretive anthropological studies contrasting two cultures may say that in one of them having fun is a highly meaningful activity, whereas in the other one working is far more meaningful than having fun. Designers of cross-cultural computer-supported collaborative systems may have to take such differences in consideration if they have members of *both* exemplified cultures among their users. Should the system's interface concentrate on work? Should it let users see who else is online and allow them to invite any other user for a casual chat when they feel like? How would more *talkative* users from one culture react to a *Do not disturb* sign attached to the picture of some online co-worker? These are instances of cross-cultural issues in human communication that naturally percolate to technology being used in cross-cultural contexts. Hence our interest in dealing with them.

Geertz's perspective on cultural anthropology can be combined seamlessly with semiotic theories that support the research presented in this book. In general, semioticians agree that culture is "a communal system of meanings that provides the means for human beings to translate their instincts, urges, needs, and other propensities into representational and communicative structures" [6].

The work of other anthropologists specifically interested in intercultural communication, such as Hall and his followers [15–18], can also support HCI designers in building cross-cultural systems. From a narrower perspective than the one taken by Geertz, Hall's main contributions focus on communicative encounters between people with different cultural backgrounds. Viewing culture as matter of communication, Hall [17, 18] examines the relation between the context of the message and its effectiveness to communicate cultural content in intercultural communication. The more rules and cultural codes are explicitly contextualized, the higher the chances of mutual understanding of cultural content.

Most of the HCI research on culture carried out in the last 15–20 years has been trying to understand the impact of culture on the users' experience and to frame cultural issues in the process of HCI design [5, 10, 12, 29, 35, 36]. There have been studies proposing alternatives to existing design and evaluation processes or completely new solutions to accommodate cultural factors in conceptualizing and building user interfaces for cross-cultural systems [3, 4, 21, 26, 28, 31].

The most prominent approach in this context has been internationalization-localization (Int-Loc) [10, 19, 23, 25]. Internationalization is the process of creating a base design that can be easily adapted for various international markets [13]. With internationalization, the core functionality of the system is separated from localized interface details (text, numbers, dates, etc.), whereas with localization, the interface of a system is customized for a particular audience (not only through language translation, but also through technical, national, and cultural features of the system) [23].

Hofstede's [20] research has been particularly appealing to adopters of the Int-Loc approach. Generalized personality traits transformed into cultural features provide powerful design orientation for international and localized websites, for example. Is this incompatible with the Semiotic Engineering view that we present in this book? Not really, but we intend to show how the switch to an interpretive view can open new possibilities for Int-Loc and beyond.

Generalized views of the *audience* are common in mass communication processes. Yet, one of the promises of ICT is to achieve much finer segmentation of the audience, aiming even at *personalized* media communication as is the case of many interactive TV projects [2]. Our Semiotic Engineering perspective helps going in this direction, by framing human-computer interaction as computer-mediated human communication, where individual competence and interpretations can be brought to bear in innovative ways.

The first step in organizing intercultural metacommunication is to define the kinds of systems that we target at this stage of our research. Very explicitly we are interested in *systems whose designers want to expose cultural diversity*. In other words, we address design contexts where cultural diversity is intentionally included in the

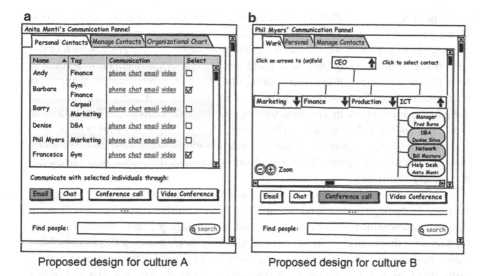

Proposed design for culture A   **Proposed design for culture B**

Fig. 1.4 System modules with culturally-adapted interface designs (**a**) Proposed design of culture A. (**b**) Proposed design of culture B

designers' metacommunication message to the users. For a very brief illustration of what this choice amounts to, let us go back to the Computer Supported Cooperative Work (CSCW) application quickly mentioned above. We are talking about a cross-cultural system whose members come from two different cultures: culture A where social relations are more meaningful than work relations; and culture B where the opposite is the case. Information coming from interpretive anthropological studies may have convinced the designers that the dialog design in Fig. 1.4a is good for culture A and that the one in Fig. 1.4b is good for culture B. Both dialog designs refer to group communication controls to be made available in our hypothetical CSCW application.

Notice that the design on the left-hand side (Fig. 1.4a) is supposed to depict "Anita Monti's" interface, and the one on the right-hand side (Fig. 1.4b) is supposed to depict "Phil Myers'" interface. According to the signs we see in the figure, Anita and Phil communicate with each other. However, Anita comes from a culture where personal communication for social purposes has been found to be more meaningful than work-related communication. Evidence from anthropological studies shows that even work-related communication in culture A is framed within the context of personally meaningful communication. Likewise, in culture A social protocols tend to be more informal and closer than in culture B.

Taking this knowledge into consideration, HCI designers can guess that users located in places where cultures A or B prevail will work better if meaningful social protocols are supported by the system. The challenge, of course, rises when users from these different cultures have to communicate and work *with each other*. Possibly, Phil's work-oriented no-nonsense style when communicating with Anita will give her the impression that he is unfriendly and pedantic. Anita's warm and chatty style, in turn, may give Phil the impression that she is intrusive and disrespectful. If we look at the interface signs chosen to compose the metacommunication message in Fig. 1.4a, b, we see that the strategy of designing *for each*, which in this case is the result of using Int-Loc to build the system, actually *encourage* Anita to treat Phil as a member of her own culture, and vice-versa. Note that they appear in each other's list of contacts, along with other members of their own respective culture. In particular, see that contacts with tag "Gym" and "Carpool" in Fig. 1.4a mean that these individuals are *physically* close to Anita. Anita and Phil will have to learn to overcome occasional mutual misunderstandings using their own resources, trying to circumvent cultural blunders whose occurrence *the system* may have unintentionally facilitated.

Designing for all, in search of a single universal interface with the best compromise between including all meaningful features from all cultures or only those features that are meaningful for all cultures, cannot completely prevent cultural blunders. Neither does this strategy help the users in detecting them, avoiding them or resolving them. Isolating cultural differences, as is often the result of localization, and neutralizing them, as is often the result of internationalization, does not *expose* cultural diversity to the users in the way we are interested in being able to do.

The first step toward the semiotic engineering of cross-cultural systems, whose designers intend to communicate cultural diversity, is to organize the designer's choices with respect to how they want users from one culture to approach meanings from another culture. These meanings can be conveyed by the users themselves (in communication through email, chat, conference calls or video conferences, for instance) and by the system's interface (i.e. by the designers, through the specific signs that they choose to include in their metacommunication message to users). Because the latter may clearly affect the former, we began our research by investigating the organization of the *designers*' communication about cultural diversity. In the future, we will investigate how the users' communication with each other unfolds in systems specifically designed in accordance with various metacommunication strategies.

CVM constitute a conceptual tool that cross-cultural systems' designers can use to organize cultural metacommunication choices while composing their message to users. The whole process begins with deciding what the top-level design intent is and which perspective on culture and intercultural contact is best. From such decisions various other choices regarding cultural content follow. Choices include the kinds of communicative strategies and signification systems that will more effectively and efficiently convey the designer's message.

CVM lead HCI designers to conceive cross-cultural systems *as a journey* and users as *travelers* and, in addition, to decide whether it is appropriate to explicitly expose users to other cultures and how. Figure 1.5 shows the distinct perspectives brought by each metaphor. The five metaphors are plotted upon a continuum of cultural approximation established with reference to a presumed user's culture [30].

In Semiotic Engineering terms, the adoption of each metaphor leads HCI designers to tell (or not tell) different things about cultural diversity. At both extremes there is no mediated cultural contact. At one end, ***the domestic traveler metaphor*** leads

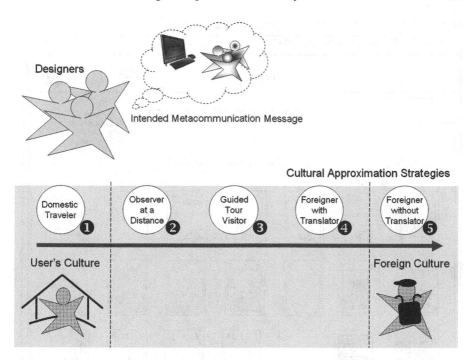

Fig. 1.5 CVM for organizing intercultural metacommunication

the users into cultural isolation, since they are not exposed to material explicitly referenced to a foreign culture. Design intends to conceal every possible intercultural contact with signs from a foreign culture. At the other end, *the foreigner without translator metaphor* leads the users' experience to complete cultural immersion, because they are fully exposed to a foreign culture's language and cultural practices, without translations or explanations about foreign interface signs and interaction forms.

In between these two extremes, however, there are three metaphors marking different levels of cultural mediation: *the observer at a distance*, *the guided tour visitor* and *the foreigner with translator metaphors. The observer at a distance metaphor's* intended effect on the organization of interactive discourse is to offer only allusive references to a foreign culture. The users' culture dominates the interface signs and interaction forms. With *the guided tour visitor metaphor* design explicitly guides the users as they experience selected aspects of a foreign culture through interface signs and interaction forms borrowed from this culture's language(s) and social practices. Finally, *the foreigner with translator metaphor's* intended effect is to allow users to directly experience the cultural practices from a foreign culture through interface signs and interaction forms; only the users' native language is retained as a reference to his native culture.

The effect of these metaphors, as further chapters in this book will show in detail, is remarkably *epistemic*. While asking themselves how they want to expose foreign

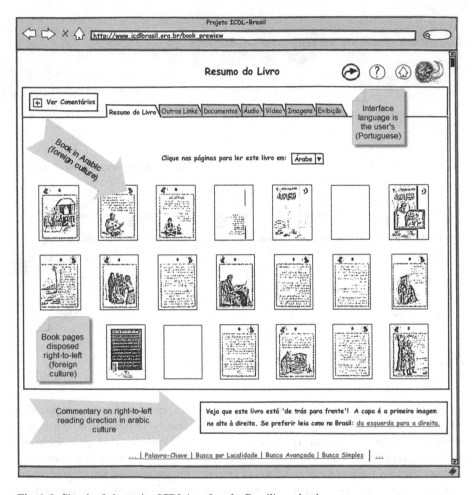

Fig. 1.6 Sketch of alternative ICDL interface for Brazilian school

culture to users *through system domain signs*, the designers raise their awareness of the role of cultural knowledge not only in successful intercultural communication from the users' point of view, but also – as our case study clearly shows – from the designers' own. Evidence collected in CVM-supported cross-cultural systems design and evaluation tasks during an extended case study tells that participants suddenly became aware of their *own* cultural values (and biases) for building and assessing top-level metacommunication strategies.

For an example of how these metaphors can materialize in systems interfaces, take Fig. 1.6. It shows a design mockup for a culturally-adapted interface of the International Children's Digital Library (ICDL) to be used by Brazilian lower school children. ICDL allows users from all over the world, children in particular, to read digital books in more than 60 different languages.[4] One of the interface challenges that we explored in a binational research collaboration program with the ICDL research group at the University of Maryland[5] is how to prevent users from getting lost in the labyrinth of foreign languages that they are exposed to.

In Fig. 1.6, the design follows *the guided tour visitor metaphor*. The users see the interface in their own language (Portuguese), but they make vivid contact with elements of the Arabic culture (where the book being shown comes from). The designers' interactive discourse *calls the users attention* to cultural diversity, introducing static, dynamic and metalinguistic signs referring to the Arabic culture. For instance, the book pages are displayed in the opposite direction as it should be in Brazilian culture (a static sign). If Brazilian users click on one page and begin to browse the book, animation will *turn the pages backwards* (a dynamic sign of how books are manipulated in the foreign culture). Moreover, designers explicitly include text (see bottom of the screen) commenting on this reading practice difference between the two cultures (a metalinguistic sign). Notice, finally, that this style of design is *neither* localized, *nor* internationalized. It is the result of intentional effort to promote the user's contact with a foreign culture, which leads us back to the beginning of this introduction and to our final remarks.

1.4   On the Content and Structure of This Book

This book is targeted at HCI researchers and reflective professionals who are interested in the design of cross-cultural systems that intentionally *expose* users to cultural diversity. These systems become increasingly important in a world where mutual understanding and tolerance among people from (and within) all countries is widely considered the key to a safer future [34].

Our contribution springs from Semiotic Engineering [8], a theory of HCI that views human-computer interaction as a twofold computer-mediated communication process involving systems designers and systems users. Semiotic Engineering has the effect of making designers *participate* in interaction and thus be led into designing not only the users' communication with 'the system', but also – and importantly – *their own* style, spectrum, structure, purpose, modes and means of communication with users through the system's interface (which represents designers at interaction time). We do not propose any method to elicit cultural variables from user communities. Rather, we assume that ethnographic studies carried out by cultural anthropologists in the users' communities will provide the cultural content that designers must then communicate to users.

Semiotic Engineering investigates signs and meanings in designer-to-user metacommunication, that is, communication about how, when, where and why to

---

[4] http://en.childrenslibrary.org/about/fastfacts.shtml

[5] http://www.icdl-br.inf.puc-rio.br/

communicate with the system. Designers adopting our theory are thus necessarily interested in *positioning* themselves in face of the users' needs and expectations, as well as in the face of needs and expectations from other stakeholders involved in the construction and deployment of interactive computer technologies.

The semiotic engineering of cross-cultural systems is especially challenging, given the ethical choices involved in selecting which elements from different cultures to expose to members of *other* cultures, and how. It is, as we have shown in this introduction, a clear case of the situation Latour has invoked in his address to designers in 2008. We attempt to help designers in exposing "an impression of the controversies and the many contradicting stakeholders" [22, p. 9], giving voice to diverse cultural values through a system's interface.

Our first step in trying to respond to Latour's challenge is CVM. At this stage of our research, the five cultural viewpoint metaphors have been applied only to the organization of the top-level strategy of designer-to-user metacommunication about cultural diversity. We haven't yet investigated user inter-communication in cross-cultural systems, especially because we believe that designer-to-user meta-communication is likely to affect considerably the computer-mediated communication among users. Thus, before we have a deeper understanding of the former, we don't think we are prepared to investigate the latter.

The next chapters of this book elaborate on the ideas briefly presented in this introduction. Chapter 2 discusses culture, Semiotics and Semiotic Engineering. Chapter 3 presents CVM in detail. Chapter 4 presents an extensive two-phase case study that we carried out to assess how *meaningful* CVM are in cross-cultural HCI design and evaluation contexts. Finally, Chap. 5 discusses our findings and presents our current conclusions and thoughts about the future of CVM.

References

1. Andersen, P. B. (1997). *A theory of computer semiotics: Semiotic approaches to construction and assessment of computer systems* (2nd ed.). Cambridge: Cambridge University Press.
2. Ardissono, L., Kobsa, A., & Maybury, M. T. (2010). *Personalized digital television: Targeting programs to individual viewers*. Heidelberg: Springer.
3. Barber, W., & Badre, A. (1998). Culturability: The merging of culture and usability. In *Proceedings of the 4th conference on human factors & the web*. Basking Ridge: Online publi- cation. Available at http://www.research.att.com/conf/hfweb/proceedings/barber/index.htm. Last visited in Jan 2012.
4. Bourgues-Waldegg, P., & Scrivener, S. A. R. (1998). Meaning, the central issue in cross-cultural HCI design. *Interacting with Computers, 9*(3), 287–309.
5. Curzon, P., Wilson, J., & Whitney, G. (2005). Successful strategies of older people for finding information. *Interacting with Computers, 17*(6), 660–671.
6. Danesi, M., & Perron, P. (1999). *Analyzing cultures: An introduction and handbook*. Bloomington: Indiana University Press.
7. de Souza, C. S. (1993). The semiotic engineering of user interface languages. *International Journal of Man-Machine Studies, 39*(5), 753–773.
8. de Souza, C. S. (2005). *The semiotic engineering of human-computer interaction*. Cambridge, MA: The MIT Press.

9. de Souza, C. S., & Leitão, C. F. (2009). *Semiotic engineering methods for scientific research in HCI*. San Francisco: Morgan and Claypool Publishers.
10. Del Gado, E., & Nielsen, J. (1996). *International user interfaces*. New York: Wiley.
11. Dourish, P. (2001). *Where the action is: The foundations of embodied interaction*. Cambridge, MA: The MIT Press.
12. Duncker, E. (2002). Cross-cultural usability of the library metaphor. In *Proceedings of the 2nd ACM/IEEE-CS joint conference on digital libraries* (pp. 223–230). Portland/New York: ACM Press.
13. Fernandes, T. (1995). *Global interface design: A guide to designing international user interfaces*. San Diego: Academic Press Professional.
14. Geertz, C. (1973). *The interpretation of cultures: Selected essays*. New York: Basic Books.
15. Hall, E. T. (1959). *The silent language*. New York: Anchor Books.
16. Hall, E. T. (1966). *The hidden dimension*. New York: Doubleday.
17. Hall, E. T. (1976). *Beyond culture*. New York: Doubleday.
18. Hall, E. T., & Hall, M. R. (1990). *Understanding cultural differences*. Yarmouth: Intercultural Press.
19. Hisham, S., & Edwards, A. D. (2007). Incorporating culture in user-interface: A case study of older adults in Malaysia. In *Proceedings of the eighteenth conference on hypertext and hypermedia* (pp. 145–146). New York: ACM.
20. Hofstede, G. H. (1984). *Culture's consequences: International differences in work-related values*. London: Sage Publications.
21. Irani, L. C., & Dourish, P. (2009, February). Postcolonial interculturality. In *Proceedings of the 2009 international workshop on Intercultural collaboration* (IWIC '09). ACM, New York, NY, USA, 249–252.
22. Latour, B. (2009). A cautious Prometheus? A few steps toward a philosophy of design (with special attention to Peter Sloterdijk). In *Networks of design: Proceedings of the 2008 annual international conference of the design history society* (pp. 2–10). Falmouth/Boca Raton: University College Falmouth/Universal Publishers.
23. Marcus, A. (2002). Global and intercultural user-interface design. In J. Jacko & A. Sears (Eds.), *The human-computer interaction handbook* (pp. 441–463). Mahwah: Lawrence Erlbaum Associates.
24. Nadin, M. (1988). Interface design and evaluation – Semiotic implications. In H. R. Hartson & D. Hix (Eds.), *Advances in human-computer interaction 2* (pp. 45–100). Norwood: Ablex.
25. Nielsen, J. (1990). *Designing user interfaces for international use*. New York: Elsevier.
26. Nielsen, J. (1990). Usability testing of international interfaces. In J. Nielsen (Ed.), *Designing user interfaces for international use*. New York: Elsevier.
27. Norman, D. A. (1986). Cognitive engineering. In D. A. Norman & S. W. Draper (Eds.), *User centered systems design* (pp. 31–62). Hillsdale: Laurence Erlbaum.
28. Russo, P., & Boor, S. (1993). How fluent is your interface?: designing for international users. In *Proceedings of the INTERACT '93 and CHI '93 conference on Human factors in computing systems* (CHI '93). ACM, New York, NY, USA, 342–347.
29. Sakala, L. (2009). *Participatory design in a cross-cultural design context*. Master thesis, University of Joensuu. Retrieved March, 2011 in: ftp://www.cs.joensuu.fi/pub/Theses/2009_MSc_Sakala_Lomanzi.pdf.
30. Salgado, L. C. C., de Souza, C. S., & Leitão, C. F. (2011). Using metaphors to explore cultural perspectives in cross-cultural design. In P. Rau (Ed.), *Internationalization, design and global development* (Vol. 6775, pp. 94–103). Berlin/Heidelberg: Springer.
31. Shen, S., Wooley, M., & Prior, S. (2006). Towards culture-centred design. *Interacting with Computers, 18*(4), 820–852.
32. Spool, J. M., & Schaffer, E. M. (2005, April 2–7). The great debate: Can usability scale up?. In *CHI '05 extended abstracts on human factors in computing systems* (pp. 1174–1175). Portland/New York: ACM.
33. Svanaes, D. (2012). Philosophy of interaction. In S. Mads & R. F. Dam (Eds.), *Encyclopedia of HCI*. Interaction-Design.org. Online at http://www.interaction-design.org/encyclopedia/philosophy_of_interaction.html. Last visited on Feb 2012.

34. UNESCO. (2011). *The United Nations Educational, Scientific and Cultural Organization.* http://www.unesco.org/new/en/culture/themes/cultural-diversity/. Last visited on Dec 2011.
35. Vatrapu, R. (2008). Cultural considerations in computer supported collaborative learning. *Research and Practice in Technology Enhanced Learning, 3*(2), 159–201.
36. Vatrapu, R., & Suthers, D. (2010). Intra- and inter-cultural usability in computer supported collaboration. *Journal of Usability Studies, 5*(4), 172–197.
37. Winograd, T., & Flores, F. (1986). *Understanding computers and cognition: A new foundation for design.* Reading: Addison-Wesley.

Chapter 2
Semiotic Engineering and Culture

Abstract This chapter presents the gist of Semiotic Engineering theory and the necessary concepts in it to understand our cultural approach. We also examine some well-established semiotic and anthropological definitions of culture according to interpretive and non-predictive perspectives. By adopting an interpretive definition of culture, Semiotic Engineering research on this topic focuses on systems whose designers want to communicate cultural diversity to users. We use this theory's ontology to map out and frame the portion of cultural interaction design space in which we are interested and to define relevant elements in the organization of culture-sensitive interactive discourse produced by systems' designers.

Influenced by pioneering semiotic approaches to computing and HCI [1, 2, 31, 38, 50], Semiotic Engineering was first proposed in the early 1990s as a semiotic approach to designing interface languages [11]. At the time, concepts of Eco's Semiotics [18] served as theoretical reference to build a framework to understand and explain HCI design issues in new ways. Over the years, instead of an *application* of semiotic concepts and perspectives to HCI, Semiotic Engineering evolved to a semiotic *theory of* HCI [14]. The theory is rooted in Peirce's [43] and Eco's [18] work, but its distinctive unit of investigation, its own set of articulated concepts and scientific methods have been precisely defined. Since 2010, in response to cultural challenges brought about by globalization, our research has systematically focused on cultural issues and on the potential of Semiotic Engineering to contribute to culture-sensitive interaction with/through computer systems.

In this chapter, we firstly present Semiotic Engineering concepts that are necessary to understand our cultural approach. Then we briefly explore some of the existing semiotic and anthropological definitions of culture [10, 18, 21, 22, 24–27], looking at how they help Semiotic Engineering to advance our understanding of culture-sensitive interaction in human-computer interaction.

L.C.C. Salgado et al., *A Journey Through Cultures: Metaphors for Guiding the Design of Cross-Cultural Interactive Systems*, Human–Computer Interaction Series, DOI 10.1007/978-1-4471-4114-3_2, © Springer-Verlag London 2013

2.1   An Overview of Semiotic Engineering Theory

Along with other semiotic approaches [1, 2, 19, 31, 38, 50], Semiotic Engineering [12–14] views computers as media. This perspective emphasizes the fact that computers mediate communication between people and that software is a piece of communication sent from its producers to its consumers through the system's interface. All semiotic approaches to HCI have in common the view that human-computer interaction is actually a particular kind of computer-mediated communication.

Compared to other semiotic approaches, Semiotic Engineering makes a fundamental step forward with the concept of *designer-to-user metacommunication*, which constitutes its primary unit of investigation. The concept refers to the idea that designers are legitimate participants (interlocutors) in the communication process that takes place through the system's interface. In Semiotic Engineering, therefore, the kind of computer-mediated communication process that takes place in what is conventionally referred to as *human-computer interaction* always involves a triad of communicators: *designer, system and user*. Both designers and users are engaged in the same metacommunication process. Designers communicate to users their design vision and assumptions, their design choices, what the produced software does and why, how it can be used, etc. Since this piece of communication is achieved as users interact with the system, the designers' message to users is actually an instance of metacommunication – communication about their own message, that is, communication about how, when, where, why and for what purposes to communicate with the system.

The communication between designers and users is neither synchronous nor direct, since designers are not present at interaction time. They talk to users through the system's interface, which is called *the designer's deputy* in Semiotic Engineering. The interface actually represents the designers and tells the users what the designers mean to communicate. As just mentioned above, the metacommunication message from designers is received and unfolded as users interact with the system. The entire process is depicted in Chap. 1 (see Sect. 1.2, Fig. 1.3, p. 7). In Fig. 2.1 we emphasize only the three interlocutors involved in and brought together by metacommunication at interaction time. The first is the designer – the metacommunication's *sender*, the one who plans, elaborates and implements his message in the form of computer software. The designer, however, cannot deliver his own message directly. The second interlocutor of the process, the system's interface, represents the designer at interaction time. It plays the designer's role in computer-mediated communication, as the designer's deputy, and delivers the entire metacommunication message to users. Finally, the users are the receivers of the message. They get it through various communication channels (audio, video, images, text, interface controls, etc.), interpret it and communicate back with the system according to the possibilities and alternatives they see in it.

Bringing designers, users and systems' interfaces together under a single theoretical framework is a fundamental and distinctive contribution of Semiotic Engineering. It helps HCI practitioners to go beyond the mere application of semiotic concepts

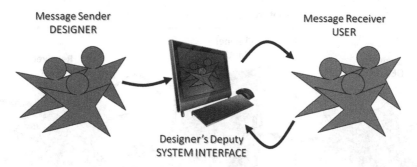

Fig. 2.1 Interlocutors involved in metacommunication in HCI

to HCI and into *thinking* human-computer interaction as a very specific phenomenon to be studied with the aid of very specific concepts, methods and tools. An ontology especially created to identify participants in human-computer situations as well as their corresponding roles contributes to defining more precisely the object of interest of HCI in general and the unit of investigation of Semiotic Engineering in particular.

At this point, we see clearly that Semiotic Engineering focuses on communication (rather than learning and memorization, for instance). Besides, we should note that this theory assigns a fundamentally important active role to HCI designers at interaction time. This does not mean that users and their role are any less important. It means that *both* roles are critically important for human-computer interaction to be fully achieved. Other theories and approaches [37, 40, 41] emphasize solely the users' role in human-computer interaction and do it very well. Semiotic Engineering brings up a new perspective and aims explicitly at focusing on how designers communicate their point of view to users, telling them why and how they intend to improve the users' lives, give them a new set of possibilities to explore [14] and so on.

The decision to attend to the designer's role and activities during interaction is consistent with Latour's views on design [35] discussed in Chap. 1 (see Sect. 1.1, p. 2). Viewing themselves as senders of the metacommunication message, designers engage in a reflective and interpretive task. Their design is about how *they* are going to tell users what *they* have to say. Designers express (consciously or not) their particular vision about the users' problem or possibilities, their corresponding solutions and alternatives, implied social values, cultural biases and even political and moral issues that may surreptitiously emerge from interaction patterns and choice of interface representations. This perspective reveals two sides of the HCI design activity, a technical engineering task of and a social activity with various kinds of effects and consequences.

The diversity of HCI perspectives, theories and emphases shows the complexity of human-computer interaction per se [13, 14, 42] and underlines the fact that all are partial and biased. Luckily, they may complement each other, helping us to have better understanding of the different facets of a complex phenomenon. As mentioned in Chap. 1 (see Sect. 1.2, p. 4), such is the case with Cognitive Engineering [40]

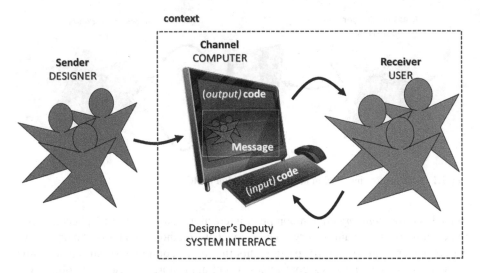

Fig. 2.2   The semiotic engineering design space

and Semiotic Engineering [12], for example. Precisely because they are partial accounts, they support HCI researchers and practitioners in identifying, separating, framing, relating and thus understanding in greater depth a host of important HCI issues.

By formulating with greater precision its unit of investigation, Semiotic Engineering can identify distinctive characteristics in designer-to-user metacommunication compared to communication in natural contexts. The theory uses Jakobson's model of communication [30] to structure the design space for semiotic activity and organize the metacommunication process. Jakobson identifies six elements in communication – context, sender, receiver, message, code and channel – and defines specific functions achieved when communication is centered on them.

Thus, in metacommunication the designer is the *sender*, the user is the *receiver*, and the computer is the *channel*. The *message* is the system's interface, which is encoded in computational *codes* and delivered though interaction (during which *it* also plays the role of a proxy for its original sender, the designer). *Context* is the wide range of situations where interaction takes place and the metacommunication process unfolds [12]. The design space therefore represents and connects each one of the six elements about which designers must make decisions, with special attention to the multiple roles played by the system's interface: a top-level message (which designers send to users) and also the sender and receiver of lower-level messages exchanged with users during interaction. The *semiotic engineering* of human-computer interaction thus amounts to the design and construction of meta-communication discourse (see Fig. 2.2).

Differently from what happens with communication in natural settings, in human-computer interaction, all the system's (i.e. the designer's deputy's) communicative turns and paths must have been previously defined by its designers and implemented in computer programs by its developers [13, 14]. The designers' semiotic processes determine the system's meaning, which is then represented by interface language constructs. Thus, the system interface consists of *interactive discourse*, the computational representation of all and only the conversations between the designer's deputy and the users that designers have selected, planned for and organized. Mutual understanding between designers and users (through systems) is possible (at interaction time) if there are shared meanings in the designers' and users' asynchronous semiotic processes of interpretation and representation of elements related to the system's domain and the actual context of interaction.

Peirce's [43] and Eco's [18] Semiotics provide at least three important concepts included in the Semiotic Engineering ontology: sign, signification and communication. These concepts are necessary to the understanding of the engineering process of interactive discourse. According to Peirce [43], a *sign* is anything that somebody takes to stand for something else, in some respect or capacity. Nothing is a sign unless it is interpreted by somebody (regardless of the results produced by such interpretation). According to Eco [18], *signification* is the process through which certain systems of signs are established as a result of social and cultural conventions adopted by interpreters and producers of such signs. Finally, *communication* is the process through which, for a variety of interpersonal purposes and effects, sign producers express intended meanings by exploring the possibilities of existing signification systems and occasionally introducing innovative signs (e.g. neologisms) or sign usage (e.g. creative figures of speech). Eco's Semiotics also distinguishes three fundamental elements in communication: *intent* (what you want to achieve with communication), *content* (what information you communicate) and *expression* (what forms and means of communication you choose).

Back to the interactive discourse engineering process, a system's interface signifies (or expresses) the design *intent* by means of a finite set of elements and structures that are specifically associated with a range of systems states and behavior. The interface thus contains a *purposefully designed signification system*, in which certain kinds of *expressions* are deliberated associated to certain kinds of *content* in order to support communication and achieve the design *intent*. Unlike face-to-face interaction, the system's interface language, its inventory of signs and sign combinations, are previously and exhaustively specified in a highly selective process that constrains communication to an exclusive range of possibilities. This includes not only the full specification (and implementation) of well-known formal language dimensions (vocabulary, syntax and semantics) but also, and particularly important in our case, the full specification of various speakers' roles, conversation contexts, speech acts and their corresponding effect, conversational rules and other pragmatic elements required to achieve the design intent.

We can thus see the inherent tension between human communication processes and computer-mediated metacommunication lying right at the core of HCI. Computer signification systems are selectively created by humans (the designers) and fully programmed into computer artifacts. They are created to support the users' interpretation and communication with as much ease and flexibility as possible. However, since they must be effectively and efficiently computable, compared to natural signification systems, interface signification systems fail to exhibit important characteristics. For example, unlike humans, interface languages encoded into computer artifacts will always generate the same (range of) mechanical interpretations for each and every representation in the program. Moreover, because of the inherent variability of program implementations and the semantic variations imposed by each system's domain of application, among other factors, each interface language is *arbitrary* (i.e. the result of intensively selective processes) and *unique* (i.e. different from all other interface languages, in spite of stylistic similarities and shared components). In other words, every time a user begins to use a new system he must learn a new language or, more precisely, in view of the theory being exposed, expand his pre-existing signification system in order to include new signs or sign variations.

Another point of tension is that the users' interpretation and sense making triggered by interface signs are open-ended (like any other human semiotic process in natural contexts) they can evolve in totally unpredictable directions motivated by unexpected contingencies or boosted by sheer creativity and imagination. However, the communicative process by which users talk back to the system is limited by computationally implemented signification systems. Therefore users must express meanings in accordance with the constraints imposed by selective vocabulary, syntax, semantics and pragmatics, taken both in the conventional sense (i.e. as linguistic components) and extended sense (i.e. as components of visual, gestural, or other signification system that is symbolically *encoded* in computer programs). Users' successful interaction with systems supposes that they have the ability to express their communicative intent in one of the anticipated ways implemented in each system. Of course, outside this highly constrained human-computer communication channel that supports exchanges during interaction, users can interpret systems' signs in whichever way they wish. For example, nothing prevents that they *interpret* full screen visualization supported by a text editor *as* a presentation tool and end up producing slide shows with text editors. Most probably this is a totally unanticipated (and arguably wrong) interpretation of text editor designers' intent. Yet, as long as the user-system communication required achieving such peculiar effect is congruent with the underlying system's linguistic specification, all works well.

Semiotic Engineering thus specifically investigates the nature, the structure, the processes, the context, the effects and conditions of metacommunication discourse. Conversations between designers and users at design time, although critically important and useful as input to successful organization and engineering of final metacommunication discourse, do not constitute an object of investigation for Semiotic Engineering. Other theories and HCI approaches are aptly dedicated to doing it with excellent results [16, 37, 39].

The way how designers represent *themselves* as producers and senders of interactive discourse is essentially important in Semiotic Engineering. In spite of the fact that whatever a system's interface communicates is actually its *designers'* communication, designers must not necessarily build anthropomorphic interfaces. They may represent themselves in different guises [12]: as machines (that *speak* through panels, buttons, controls, dials, etc.), as physical objects like file boxes, address books, and others (that *speak* through their states and representational affordances), as humanoids (that *speak* through pseudo-natural languages and other human characteristics like affect, for instance), among others. Depending on the design intent, message content and users' profile, some representations will work better than others.

In order to illustrate the designer's process of creating their representation of *self*, let us use a simple hypothetical scenario where a designer wants to build a culinary website. As a result of previous elicitation steps in the design process, let us assume that the designer knows that website users are very busy young people who love to cook and can do it well. When looking for new dishes, they like to search the Internet to get new ideas and dish recipes. They are happy with brief how-to-cook guides, with very little details and explanations. In this case, the designer's *self* might be represented as a file box with classified recipes inside may be perfectly appropriate. Users should be able to search and browse recipes supported by good (fast and smart) search engines and classification mechanisms, easy bookmarking and annotation features, and so on. Less is more, in this case. However, if the targeted users were children, just beginning to learn how to cook, a humanoid representation of the designer's *self* might be a better option. He would thus be able to talk about food, show interesting videos to teach cooking tasks and even simulate an interactive coaching process to support the users as they bake a cake. The designers would be able to talk to users and even answer a few questions while they selected and mixed ingredients, put the cake in the oven, for example.

The next important element to take into account while organizing interactive discourse to achieve good metacommunication is *what to tell users through interface*. From a top-level perspective, regardless of domain- and task-dependent variables, interactive discourse has to communicate the following to users:

- What the designers know about the users (i.e. the designers' interpretation of who the users are, what they wish and/or need to do, in which preferred ways and context, why, etc.), as well as what they know about *their own* goals, needs, expectations and abilities as designers.
- How designers have decided to respond to users' needs and expectations, i.e. the designers' depiction of how the system is, how it works and why.
- What values are present in the system, i.e. why and how the system improves the users' lives or offers new possibilities for users to explore, and what effects are expected.

In order to support designers' analysis and synthesis about the content above, Semiotic Engineering summarizes it in a general schema of designer-to-user message – called the metacommunication template – which says:

> Here is our understanding of who you are, what we've learned you want or need to do, in which preferred ways, and why. This is the system that we have therefore designed for you, and this is the way you can or should use it in order to fulfill a range of purposes that fall within this vision.

The metacommunication template sums up, in a top-level perspective, what designers are communicating to users. The first person "I" refers to the designer or to the design team, and the second person "you" refers collectively to the targeted user population. Two important points must be emphasized again regarding this template, or, more appropriately, the designer-user metacommunication process that the template represents [14]: (a) the role of the receiver is as important as that of the sender; and (b) the metacommunication happens independently of the designers' or users' degree of awareness that they are communicating with each other.

The organization of interactive discourse in a top-level perspective is supported by the definition of the interlocutors involved in HCI metacommunication, as well as by the construction of the metacommunication message guided by the top-level template (see Chap. 1, Sect. 1.2, Fig. 1.3, p. 7).

Still at a high level of abstraction, Semiotic Engineering models [4–6] help designers think and gain new knowledge about interactive discourse. These models are especially useful in formative stages of design, before the designer's communication has been fully encoded as achieved interface messages presented in the system's interface. Semiotic Engineering's Modeling Language for Interaction as Conversation – MoLIC [5, 6, 45], for instance, helps HCI practitioners to plan for all conversational exchanges in which the designer's deputy can possibly engage at interaction time. By using MoLIC to model such conversation in varying levels of abstraction, the designers can explore alternative design views and produce multiple choices for communication with users. Of course, the full specification of the interface requires that the designers plan for detailed levels of interaction, which is the equivalent of specifying a *purposeful signification system* for metacommunication. As already mentioned, in this system, specific kinds of signs are deliberately associated with specific kinds of content in order to support successful communication of the design intent.

Because the context of HCI metacommunication is fundamentally different from natural communication, Semiotic Engineering chooses to work with different classes of signs: static, dynamic and metalinguistic signs [14]. This classification is especially productive for the analysis and design of interactive discourse. Static signs are interface signs whose meaning can be interpreted instantaneously, independently of temporal and causal relations pertaining to the ongoing metacommunication. The context of interpretation is limited to the state of interface at a single moment in time. In the Terra Culinária website[1] (see corresponding sketch in Fig. 2.3), for instance, the metacommunication is achieved mainly with static signs: numbers and drawings represent a list of hamburger ingredients created for children.

A similar preference for metacommunication with static signs is present in Jamie Oliver website[2] (see corresponding sketch in Fig. 2.4). In it there are photos, a list of ingredients and some how-to-cook tips whose interpretation can be easily achieved instantaneously.

Temporal dimensionality is the main characteristic of the second class of signs proposed by Semiotic Engineering. *Dynamic* signs are bound to temporal and causal

---

[1] http://www.terra.com.br/culinaria/criancas/salgados_02.html (as in February 2012).

[2] http://www.jamieoliver.com/recipes/other-recipes/coconut-pancakes-with-pomegranate-jewels (as in February 2012).

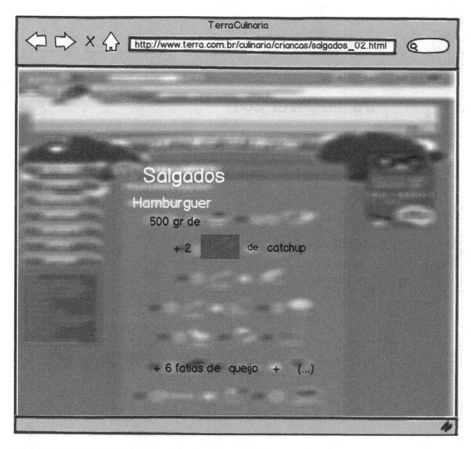

Fig. 2.3 Terra Culinária website (Hamburger recipe)

aspects of the interface. They can communicate their meaning through a series of time-dependent representations. Usually these signs can only be correctly interpreted over a number of subsequent screens or system states. Individual intermediary states (which might be taken for static signs) either fail to communicate anything at all or communicate something that must be revised after a temporal sequence is shown. This is the gist of dynamic signs; their meaning is only grasped over time (or, more precisely, they only emerge *as a sign* of what they mean after some time interval is elapsed). A change of color and font format accompanied by a change in cursor format is a commonly used dynamic sign for Web links, requiring a time interval that supports the perception of a contrast between 'before' and 'after'. Likewise, the time-dependent contrast between the states of the system before and after the user clicks on the link is a dynamic signification of what the link representation (typically some text or image) actually means. The Allrecipes website[3] (see corresponding

---

[3] http://allrecipes.com/ (as in February 2012).

Fig. 2.4 Jamie Oliver website (coconut pancakes)

sketch in Fig. 2.5) shows another example of metacommunication in culinary websites. In it, there is a "play" button inviting users to start a video that shows how to cook a ham and potato soup. The designer's choice for a video, a dynamic sign par excellence, seems to be a good option in many situations where learning from visual descriptions is easier than learning from textual instructions. For busy users, with large experience in cooking, written instructions might be better, for they would be able to skim very quickly through them in order to assess whether there is anything particularly relevant for them. But for beginners, dynamic signs are probably better, even if they take much longer to achieve their full expression through the interface.

Metalinguistic signs are static or dynamic signs that, as their name suggests, achieve a specific *recursive* function in metacommunication. They explicitly inform, illustrate or explain the meaning of *other* static and dynamic signs. In other words, they are interface signs for other interface signs. They usually come in form of help or error messages, tutorial guides, screen tips, etc.

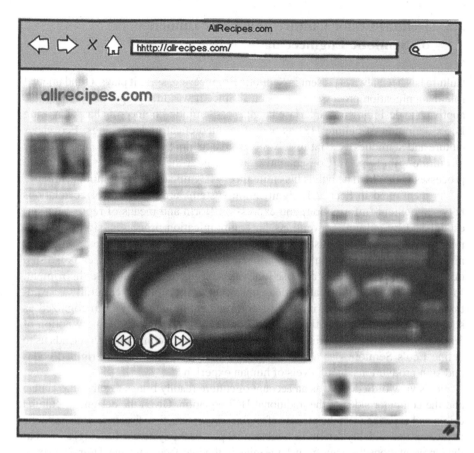

Fig. 2.5 Allrecipes.com website (homepage)

Designers define their communicative strategies by composing messages with these three kinds of signs. All the signs included in their purposeful signification system designed to achieve the intended metacommunication are basically classified as static, dynamic or metalinguistic signs. Further classifications can of course be used to organize domain-related signs, task-related signs, and so on. The top-level metacommunication message that instantiates the template presented on page 25 unfolds through various individual pieces of communication produced as users navigate the conversational paths that they choose during interaction. The complete message from the designers is programmed into the system and delivered with it. This is why it has been referred to as a "one-shot message" from designers to users. It is uncovered and discovered by the users as they interact with the designers' deputy (which is itself a crucial part of the message) and gain access to (or infer the existence of) all the designed signs.

2.2   Definitions for Culture and Their Influence on Semiotic Engineering

Culture has been always present in Semiotic Engineering, since it plays a fundamental role in signification processes and systems. Since it was first proposed as a semiotic approach to designing user interface languages, Semiotic Engineering has been using Eco's definition of culture [18] as one of its theoretical underpinnings. Eco views culture and Semiotics as so intimately related that to him Semiotics is in fact "the logic of culture" [ibid., p. 3]. Consequently, culture is at the basis of two fundamental processes with which he builds his entire theory: signification and communication.

As mentioned in Sect. 2.1, signification systems are the result of correlations between content (information) and expression (form and means of representation) established by cultural conventions. In communication processes, sign producers manipulate and explore existing signification systems in order to express intended meanings. They do so mainly with conventionalized signs, but they can also step out of established systems and use innovative signs to communicate their intent. In other words, communication does not necessarily replicate culturally conventionalized codes, but even innovative communication can only be recognized as such with reference to existing cultural conventions (otherwise the very notion of *innovation* is lost). This primacy of social conventions in communication leads us to define Eco's Semiotics as a comprehensive study of culturally-determined codes and sign productions, at all levels of human experience.

Eco's view of Semiotics as an account of culture readily brings together the human and the computer sides of the traditional HCI equation. Given the designers' cultural origin and experience, in the process of engineering interactive discourse, their semiotic influences unavoidably determine a substantial part of the system's meaning, as well as the representations that signify such meaning in the interface language. Users, however, influenced by their own cultural background, as they acquire the logic of the designed interface language, eventually face the consequences of greater or lesser cultural differences. Mutual understanding between designers and users (through the system) thus also depend on differences and similarities in both parties' cultural backgrounds.

The fundamental role of culture in Eco's Semiotics, which so extensively influences Semiotic Engineering, in itself already implies that designer-to-user metacommunication has inherently cultural dimensions. However, this is clearly not enough to support an in-depth segmented analysis of such dimensions at design and interaction time. For instance, what can we expect to see in metacommunication if designers and users come from different cultures? What can we expect to see in computer-mediated communication between users from different cultures? Or when users from one culture interact with applications whose domain belongs to a different culture (e.g. when Brazilian users interact with the National Hockey League website[4])? And what if the designers' aim is precisely to engineer *interaction discourse about culture* (as is the case with the UNESCO website, for example)?

---

[4] In Brazil, a tropical country, sports that are usually practiced on ice and snow are very little known by the population in general.

Returning to the illustrative culinary domain that we have used in previous examples, instead of just presenting recipes from different countries around the world, website designers might wish take the opportunity to communicate to users cultural food practices from the country where recipes originate. In a kind of journey through cultures, they could show typical ingredients of popular dishes in several countries, highlight important events and festivities when people from a given country eat special dishes, illustrate food utensils used in different places around the world, etc. If designers choose to do it, their design intent clearly involves promoting the users' encounter with cultural diversity. Therefore, in this case, the designer-to-user metacommunication not only has inherently cultural dimensions (as any other piece of metacommunication), but it also is *about culture*.

In order to understand and support design reasoning and decision-making when design intent explicitly involves intercultural experience, we investigated some established references in the study of culture, both in Anthropology and Cultural Semiotics. Traditionally, Anthropology is the field in which the study of cultures has been established and developed by means of appropriate ethnographic methods. Among anthropologists, it is generally accepted that the first definition of *culture* documented in print was given by Edward B. Tylor in 1871: "Culture, or civilization, taken in its broad, ethnographic sense, is that complex whole which includes knowledge, belief, art, morals, law, custom, and any other capabilities and habits acquired by man as a member of society" [47, p. 1]. From the beginning, the study of *culture* has dealt with means and meanings, interpersonal interactions and social practices.

However, as Anthropology evolved and matured as a discipline, different perspectives have been adopted by culture theorists. In 1974, Keesing [32] identified three such perspectives: cultures as adaptive systems; cultures as ideational systems (further divided into cognitive, structural and symbolic systems); and cultures as sociocultural systems. Among many elaborate challenges and implications of adopting one perspective instead of another, Keesing touches on two points that are especially relevant in this book. One is how theories of culture deal with the tension between the notion of *shared collective meanings* and the obvious *variability of individual contingent behavior*. To privilege supra-individual levels of description, analysis may come at the expense of understanding very concrete facts of life that cultural knowledge could help illuminate and perhaps improve. The other is an epistemological challenge, which Keesing developed further in later work [33]: when dealing with cultures, anthropologists *construct* the OTHER. Therefore, their description of cultural diversity is essentially an interpretation of how some individual or group is different from ME. In other words, the cultural contingency of anthropological research should always be a matter of consideration when discussing theories of culture.

Our research on cultural aspects of human-computer interaction requires, however, that we choose a consistent perspective on culture. But in so doing, we want to acknowledge the existence and the relevance of other alternatives. To this end, we quote Keesing's insightful conclusion of his 1974 paper:

> Conceiving culture as an ideational subsystem within a vastly complex system, biological, social and symbolic, and grounding our abstract models in the concrete particularities of human social life, should make possible a continuing dialectic that yields deepening understanding.

Whether in this quest the concept of culture is progressively refined, radically reinterpreted, or progressively extinguished will in the long run scarcely matter if along the way it has led us to ask strategic questions and to see connections that would otherwise have been hidden. [32, p. 94]

Among the perspectives presented by Keesing, viewing culture as a symbolic system is consistent with Eco's concept of culture, and particularly suitable to presenting conceptual metaphors to guide the *semiotic engineering* of human-computer interaction. Consequently, the theorist we choose to introduce our particular view on culture is Geertz [21, 22]. This passage from *"The interpretation of cultures"*, also quoted in Chap. 1 (see Sect. 1.3, p. 9), explicitly invokes Semiotics:

The concept of culture I espouse [...] is essentially a semiotic one. Believing, with Max Weber, that man is an animal suspended in webs of significance he himself has spun, I take culture to be those webs, and the analysis of it to be therefore not an experimental science in search of law but an interpretive one in search of meaning. It is explication I am after, construing social expressions on their surface enigmatical. [21, p. 5]

Geertz's justification for taking a semiotic perspective on culture is, moreover, remarkably close to the essence of HCI design even in the context of non-semiotic perspectives:

The whole point of a semiotic approach to culture is, as I have said, to aid us in gaining access to the conceptual world in which our subjects live so that we can, in some extended sense of the term, converse with them. [21, p. 24]

From Geertz's perspective, this kind of conversation is *not* an observation followed by the writing out a systematic set of rules named as "an ethnographic algorithm, which, if followed, would make it possible so to operate" [21, p. 11]. The interpretive anthropology proposed by Geertz stresses the importance of thinking culture in more concrete terms in order to develop scientific knowledge. One of the main risks of adopting a high-level of abstraction when defining culture (as is, for example, the case with Tyler's definition quoted above) is the implicit or explicit ambition to explain everything when using it. Cultural symbol systems cannot be elicited by applying abstract schemas to supposedly uniform patterns. Geertz's position, quoted below, emphasizes the contextual dependency of theoretical statements about culture:

As interworked systems of construable signs (what, ignoring provincial usages, I would call symbols), culture is not a power, something to which social events, behaviors, institutions, or processes can be casually attributed; it is a context, something within which they can be intelligibly – that is, thickly – described. [21, p. 14]

Theoretical statements are always closely connected to their objects. They are microscopic, non-predictable and interpretive knowledge. However, as it is expected from theoretical knowledge, they go beyond immediate perceptions and opinions, beyond a mere collection of events and facts. After all, if theoretical statements cannot, in some way or another, achieve some level of generality, then they are not theoretical. Therefore, in an interpretive anthropology perspective, previous knowledge about culture is essential to ongoing research. This is not for other researchers to begin their work from the point where previous research has stopped. Rather, the value of interpretive research lies in that researchers have more information and new (conceptual) instruments to produce their own interpretation, which is in fact a new account of the same (or of closely-related) objects and phenomena from previous research. Geertz sums up: "a study is an advance if it is more incisive – whatever that may mean – than those that preceded it; but it less stands on their shoulders than, challenged and challenging, runs by their side". [21, p. 25]

Therefore, in this view, theoretical work about culture amounts to in-depth situated symbolic interpretations of social events. Firstly, they provide means to uncover meanings and, then, they allow us to construct a system to interpret and register them. As Geertz concludes:

> Our double task is to uncover the conceptual structures that inform our subjects' acts, the 'said' of social discourse, and to construct a system of analysis in whose terms what is generic to those structures, what belongs to them because they are what they are, will stand against the other determinants of human behavior. In ethnography, the office of theory is to provide a vocabulary in which what symbolic action has to say about itself – that is, about the role of culture in human life – can be expressed [21, p. 27]

Geertz's perspective is fully consistent with Semiotic Engineering conceptions about human-computer interaction and culture, as it deals with interpretive and non-predictive knowledge and with a semiotic view of culture. Additionally, this last quote gives us an important insight about HCI research on cultural aspects in general, and about Semiotic Engineering contributions in particular. As is the case with anthropology, we also have a double task in HCI research on cultural issues. The first is to construct or adapt knowledge and methods to support the elicitation step in cross-cultural design (or to uncover the conceptual structures of the user's cultural practices). In advancing this task, the knowledge from other disciplines (as Anthropology, for example) and from other HCI theories and approaches [7, 16, 17, 29, 37–39, 44, 46, 49] are essential contributions. They competently provide data (or the means to collect them) in order to define which cultural variables must be dealt with in modeling the domain and the user profiles in culture-sensitive systems design. The second task is to design and build a culture-sensitive interaction system, based on the results achieved with the previous task. It is exactly at this point, in consistence with the interpretive anthropology perspective, that Semiotic Engineering may offer support to cross-cultural design, by providing a vocabulary and a structure to think about how to express previously elicited cultural variables in the interactive discourse communicated through a computer system's interface.

With a narrower focus than Geertz's, the contributions of Edward Hall [24–27], a twentieth century distinguished anthropologist, are also valuable in view of our needs while building interactive culture-sensitive discourse. Hall's position is also that culture studies have to be conducted in strong connection with their object and context. He proposed a narrowly-focused approach to culture, namely Intercultural Communication. It investigates situations "where people from different cultural backgrounds interact", and culture is thus defined as "the link between human beings and the means they have of interacting with others" [24, p. 213]. The contexts examined by Hall include teaching, training and organizational settings, driven by such practical goals as, for example, the development of intercultural skills and good solutions for typical communication mismatches arising in intercultural interactions.

Although Geertz and Hall seem to agree that culture studies have to be strongly related to context, Hall, as an applied anthropologist, and unlike Geertz, often proposes *principles* which compose a kind of "how-to" guide for identifying and solving micro-level intercultural communication problems. From Hall's perspective, "[inter] cultural communications are deeper and complex" and his aim is to propose conceptual tools to help us "decipher the complex unspoken rules of each culture" [27, p. 4]. To this end, he enumerates several items that can be used to understand a foreign culture, including voice, gestures, time, space, the amount of information communicated, and so on.

Hall views culture as a form of communication [24–27]. Each person involved in a communication encounter brings to it the sum of his or her own cultural background. The basic difficulty to achieve mutual understanding in communication is precisely the differences between the sender's and receiver's cultural backgrounds and way of communicating [24]. A first step to reduce the risks of misunderstanding would be to have good insight into the differences and similarities that exist between cultural backgrounds. Aiming at this goal, Hall built on Kluckhohn's categorization of two different levels of culture [34]: explicit and implicit. Explicit culture includes law, ethical codes, and other documents and things about what people can specifically talk. Implicit culture is feelings, social taboos and other things that shape our lives, but of which we are not aware of and therefore cannot put into words. Based on these two levels of culture, Hall [24, 27] defines culture as a silent language, because it "comprises some aspects that can be talked about and some that cannot" [24, p. 62]. Two categories of communication help us understand the awareness of these aspects in intercultural communication: high-context and low-context communication. The author sums up these categories:

> Context is the information that surrounds an event; it is inextricably bound up with the meaning of the event. A high context (HC) communication or message is one in which most of the information is already in the person, while very little is in the coded, explicit, transmitted part of the message. A low context (LC) communication is just the opposite, i.e. the mass of the information is vested in the explicit code. [27, p. 6]

In a high-context communication, there are many contextual elements that help people to understand the rules. As a result, much is taken for granted. In this case, intercultural communication tends to be successful when the sender delivers his message and the receiver knows the codes and rules that are not explicit in the message but are necessary for effective interpretation and communication. No explicit background information is needed. In low-context communication, in turn, very little is taken for granted in exchanged messages. This means that more explanations are needed to decrease the chances of misunderstandings. In low-context communication, the listener needs to know very little about the sender's background: he is explicitly informed about everything needed.

Hall's characterization of high and low context cultural messages is particularly interesting to refine our analysis of cross-cultural design. In a broader perspective, the design of interactive discourse, encoded in computer programs, is a low-context communication activity. As we have discussed while presenting the main concepts of Semiotic Engineering, all the designer-user conversations and all signs and structures pertaining to the signification system that supports metacommunication must be anticipated and encoded by designers at design time. These include a host of explanations, instructions and additional information (typically encoded as meta-linguistic signs) that characterize low-context communication. However, at interaction time, users do not necessarily see the big picture. The receivers' interactive experience is a gradual unfolding of designed conversations, whose rules, codes and possibilities may not be instantly anticipated or understood by the users at first encounter. In fact, depending on the communicative strategies chosen by designers, the encoded metacommunication message can be communicated to users in different levels of context. Actually, each individual round of conversation, each part of the designer's *speech*, can be elaborated at varying context levels. For example, in different portions of metacommunication, designers may feel the need to deliver explanations and rules that are appropriate for low-context messages, or trust that they can send messages in a high-context level because the users supposedly have the necessary background. This is the case in such popular applications as text editors, for instance. Communication about basic operations such as copying, pasting, changing font and paragraph format, are high context. However, when it comes to introducing cross references and building tables of content, communication is typically low context. In culture-sensitive interaction, where intercultural communication takes place, the designers' decision-making about the appropriateness of high and/or low-context communication with (and also among) users is crucial.

Geertz's and Hall's cultural approaches, briefly highlighted in this chapter, as well as Eco's conceptualization of culture, are consistent references to inform Semiotic Engineering in this new context. Once adopting their interpretive and semiotically-compatible accounts of culture, we can refine Semiotic Engineering contributions to dealing with cultural issues in HCI. But in making this foundational choice, we must acknowledge the existence of other alternatives in HCI.

HCI researchers working with culture have tended to adopt other kinds of definitions or to formulate their own. This is partly due to their effort to encapsulate interdisciplinary knowledge in a format that readers not familiar with anthropological theories of culture can understand their point. Borgman [8], for instance, writes that "culture includes race and ethnicity, as well as other variables, and is manifested in customary behaviors, assumptions and values, patterns of thinking, and communicative style" [ibid., p. 31]. Barber and Badre [3], in turn, introduce culture as follows:

> We use the word 'culture' as a means of distinguishing among the different countries and their respective websites. Our use of the term is not intended to be indicative of all the nuances and properties frequently implied by the term, but rather to permit discourse about the features that distinguish one country or region of the world from another in the electronic medium of the Web [3].

As mentioned in Chap. 1 (see Sect. 1.3, p. 9), possibly the definition most widely used in HCI has been the one proposed by Hofstede [28]: "culture is the collective programming of the mind which distinguishes the members of one category of people from another" (ibid., p. 51). This taxonomic view of culture can be used to distinguish and classify people, activities, and settings. Understandably, Hofstede's model has played an important role in HCI research whose aim is to explain and predict cultural differences [15, 20, 23, 36, 49, 51].

In Clemmensen & Roese's [9] review of a decade of journal publications about Culture and Human-Computer Interaction, culture is said to involve "country boundaries, language, cultural conventions, race and religions, not including organizational culture or other group cultures, such as different virtual environments or customer groups" [ibid., p. 4]. This is in itself a sign of the wide variety of cultural research topics discussed in HCI.

Given this heterogeneous research agenda and the different cultural approaches that serve as reference to HCI studies, at this point, it is essential to position ourselves clearly and to sum up our own cultural influences by adopting a concise and consistent definition of culture. Marcel Danesi and Paul Perron, both cultural semioticians, can help us with in this case. For them, culture is "a communal system of meanings that provides the means for human beings to translate their instincts, urges, needs, and other propensities into representational and communicative structures" [10, p. 15].

This shared system of meanings allows us to make sense of the world around us, and is referred to as the *signifying order*, "the aggregate of the signs (words, gestures, visual symbols, etc.), codes (languages, art,...) and texts (conversations, compositions, ...) that a social group creates and utilizes in order to carry out its daily life routines and to plan activities for the future" [10, p. 23]. A signifying order always mediates human understanding of the world by combing signs into patterns of representation which can be used in situated communication.

Each and every one of us has acquired a signifying order to which we have been exposed since we were born. It is not a fixed and unchanging order, but very much like the "default mode of a computer" [10, p. 70], and every human being uses his or hers for interpreting the world. Cultural groups interact based on a dominant signifying order, but there may be more than one signifying order acting inside.

As already discussed in detail above, in human-computer interaction the designers' semiotic processes determine the system's meaning, which is represented by interface language constructs. Mutual understanding between designers and users (through system) is thus possible at interaction time if they share a *signifying order*. The big challenge in cross-cultural interaction design is therefore to promote mutual understanding where *different* signifying orders are at play.

2.3 Culture-Sensitive Interaction: How Semiotic Engineering Frames Cross-Cultural Design

Semiotic Engineering is strongly committed with the challenges involving the role of Information and Communication Technologies (ITC) in the promotion of cultural diversity [48]. As discussed in Chap. 1, we are conscious of the need to generate knowledge that helps designers to develop systems that can respect and express the cultural diversity of the world, systems that invite users to take journeys through foreign cultures. Thus, Semiotic Engineering research on cultural issues begins with the design of artifacts that support culture-sensitive interaction. In other words, we focus on systems in which the designers' metacommunication intentionally includes cultural diversity.

With a Semiotic Engineering perspective, we can map out and frame design space for the cultural diversity and the potential interlocutors involved in this particular kind of metacommunication. This is achieved by combining elements of our ontology with elements of cultural knowledge. We are thus finally able to explore the possibilities for engineering the designer-to-user *discourse about culture*.

From the beginning, designing cross-cultural systems must take into consideration the needs, expectations and characteristics of intercultural encounters, both at design and interaction time. The basic difficulty to achieve mutual understanding in these encounters is the difference between the sender's (i.e. human-computer interaction designers) and receiver's (i.e. users') *signifying orders* [10].

Intercultural communication may involve encounters and promote exchanges in such different ways and contexts as:

(a) with a culturally diverse group of users (no matter whether the designers come from different cultures or not);
(b) with a culturally diverse group of designers (no matter whether users come from different cultures or not); and
(c) with a culturally diverse group of designers building cross-cultural systems for culturally diverse groups of users (a combination of the previous cases), which seems to be most common case in contemporary ICT.

Any of the above contexts may also apply when participants do not share the same cultural background as intrinsically required by the domain itself. Such is the case, for instance, of Indian designers producing systems for American users in a domain of activity where different practices are adopted by the designers' and the users' cultures.

Concrete examples of intercultural encounters at *design time* may take place in participatory design contexts (designers and users), virtual teams (people coming from different places), end-user development (users participating in a culture of software development), and so on.

At *interaction time*, intercultural contact may happen in many situations. For example, the user may make contact with a foreign culture directly by interacting with other users with Computer-Mediated Communication (CMC) technologies like instant messaging, e-mail, chat rooms, collaborative environments and so on. CMC provides opportunities for direct intercultural encounters, in the sense that contact among users, i.e. user-to-user communication, happens virtually without intermediaries. Another possibility is that the user makes contact with characteristics of a foreign culture by interacting with cross-cultural applications that explicitly communicate cultural variables (knowledge, belief, art, morals, law, custom, language, symbols, cultural conventions, communication styles and so on). The design intent

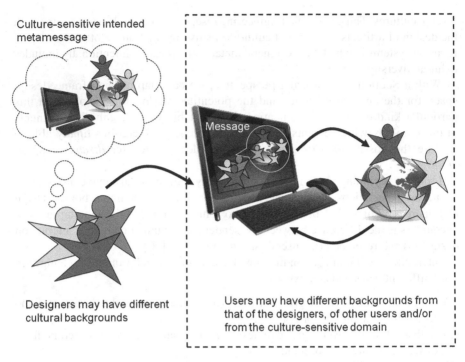

Culture-sensitive intended metamessage

Message

Designers may have different cultural backgrounds

Users may have different backgrounds from that of the designers, of other users and/or from the culture-sensitive domain

Fig. 2.6 The semiotic engineering design space including cultural diversity

of such applications is usually to expose and explore cultural diversity by providing opportunities for indirect intercultural encounters. The UNESCO[5] website is an example of systems that fall in this category.

In the light of the Semiotic Engineering ontology, the design space of this particular kind of system explicitly names the participating cultural interlocutors: the designers, the users and the system. Figure 2.6 shows that cultural diversity in this context may be spread around this space: (1) the design message may be sent by a team of designers (senders) coming from different cultures among themselves; (2) the users (receivers) may come from different cultures than the designers' (senders); (3) such users (receivers) can talk to each other through the system; and, (4) the message may refer to a multi-cultural domain and/or to some domain that presents substantial variation from one culture to another.

This preliminary mapping of cultural diversity design space for metacommunication represents and frames the field of study at the intersection between culture and HCI, to which Semiotic Engineering can contribute. It is worth remembering that the designer-to-user conversation at *design time* (not represented on Fig. 2.6) does not constitute per se an object of investigation for Semiotic Engineering. This is the first step of the design process of a cross-cultural system, the elicitation step,

[5] http://www.unesco.org/new/en/unesco/ (as in February, 2012).

in which designers gain knowledge about domain's and/or users' culture, learn and interpret their signifying orders, and elicit cultural variables to be used when engineering the cross-cultural system interface. This step (see Sect. 2.2) corresponds to what Geertz referred as the task of "uncover the cultural conceptual structures that inform our subjects' acts" [21, p. 27]. HCI approaches using ethnomethodology approaches [7, 16, 17, 29, 37–39, 44, 46] as well as anthropological studies' results are most fundamental in eliciting culture-sensitive meanings that will constitute an important portion of designer-to-user metacommunication.

Later steps in the design process, when metacommunication begins to be composed, constitute the territory for Semiotic Engineering as represented in Fig. 2.6. It concerns only the computer-encoded conversations that the designer's deputy can have with users at interaction time [14]. While in elicitation step designers learn *who* will be the receiver of their message and *what* cultural content will be communicated, in next step they will decide *how* to communicate with users through the system's interface in order to promote intercultural encounters. This refers to the organization of the designers' choices about communicative strategies, the conceptual elaboration of a computable signification system (with its corresponding signifying order) that differs from their own, the anticipation of potential conversations between the designers' deputy and users, and the definition of how their specific culture-sensitive interactive discourse will be encoded into the system.

At this point, designers must pay special attention to the potential mismatches that occur in intercultural communication because of different signifying orders that influence the process [24, 27]. Systems' domain along with the designers' and users' cultural backgrounds strongly influence decisions about the top-level metacommunication profile. For instance, designers might want to express explicitly the cultural differences between domain and users' background. In this case, they would probably choose to explain such differences by adopting an anthropomorphic representation for *themselves* at design time. For sake of illustration, in our hypothetical culinary scenario, the designer could represent himself as a Brazilian chef de cuisine character, who explains to American users how to prepare a typical Brazilian recipe. The chef would talk about typical forms of cooking in his country and contrast them with Americans cooking practices. He could occasionally take some contextual opportunity add information about his country and culture. In this illustrative description, the designer chooses to use what Hall [24] refers to as low-context communication, since all cultural content is explicit encoded into the speaker's messages. Users, as receivers, need to know very little and learn of each aspect as they journey through the foreign culture guided by the designer's deputy (the chef character) at interaction time. Alternatively, the designer could opt for high-context communication. For example, he could develop a website with a collection of videos from chefs around the world, talking to listeners from their own culture about the details of how to cook and serve typical dishes in their countries. The metacommunication in this case is not specifically tailored for users from different cultures interested in dishes from foreign countries. Users are exposed to cultural diversity, but without further explanations about potentially voluminous implicit cultural content. It is worth mentioning that we cannot dictate that high or low-context communication is always the best choice in this or that situation. The designers' message is always unique and thus contains unprecedented aspects that may introduce unexpected challenges for one type of communication or the other. What we can do is to use these notions as categories of analysis that support decision-making processes about which kinds of communication strategies and signification systems will more effectively and efficiently convey the designer's message in each particular case. As we mentioned while highlighting some of Geertz's ideas [21] on culture (see Sect. 2.2), Semiotic Engineering proposes concepts and tools that aim at connecting designers to their objects of concern; we do not propose abstract guidelines and patterns that can be *applied* by design practitioners to generate ready-made solutions to intercultural metacommunication problems.

When talking about communicative strategies to promote contact with other cultures through user-system interaction, we are actually talking about system interfaces that *mediate intercultural contact between users and signs of a foreign culture.* This chapter has shown that intercultural contact may happen not only when users themselves exchange cultural meanings with each other (e.g. in social networks), but also when users are interacting only with the system and cultural meanings are communicated by the interface itself (which represents designers at interaction time). Because the latter also affects the former, Semiotic Engineering research on culture begins with the organization of culture-sensitive interactive discourse produced by systems designers. In next chapter, we present the *Cultural Viewpoint Metaphors (CVM)*, a conceptual tool to help designers organize interactive discourse to promote cultural diversity.

References

1. Andersen, P. B. (1997). *A theory of computer semiotics: Semiotic approaches to construction and assessment of computer systems* (2nd ed.). Cambridge: Cambridge University Press.
2. Andersen, P. B., Holmqvist, B., and Jensen, J. F. (Eds.). (1993). *The computer as medium.* Cambridge: Cambridge University Press.
3. Barber, W., & Badre, A. (1998). Culturability: The merging of culture and usability. In *Proceedings of the 4th conference on human factors and the web.* (1998). Basking Ridge: Online publication. Available at http://www.research.att.com/conf/hfweb/proceedings/barber/index.htm. Last visited in January, 2012.
4. Barbosa, C. M. A. (2006). *Manas: uma ferramenta epistêmica. de apoio ao projeto da comunicação em sistemas colaborativos.* Ph.D. thesis applied to Computer Science Department, PUC-Rio, Brazil. Retrieved from http://www2.dbd.puc-rio.br/pergamum/biblioteca/php/mostrateses.php?open=1&arqtese=0210647_06_Indice.html. Last visited in February 2012.
5. Barbosa, S. D. J., & de Souza, C. S. (2001). Extending software through metaphors and metonymies. *Knowledge Based Systems, 14*(1–2), 15–27.
6. Barbosa, S. D. J., & Paula, M. G. (2003). Designing and evaluating interaction as conversation: A modeling language based on semiotic engineering. In J. Jorge, N. J. Nunes, & J. Falcão e Cunha (Eds.), *Interactive systems design, specification, and verification: 10th international workshop,* DSV-IS 2003 (pp. 16–33). Madeira Island: Lecture Notes in Computer Science.
7. Beyer, H., & Holtzblatt, K. (1998). *Contextual design: Defining customer-centered systems.* San Francisco: Morgan Kaufmann.

8. Borgman, C. L. (1992). Cultural diversity in interface design. *SIGCHI Bulletin, 24*(4), 31.
9. Clemmensen, T., & Roese, E. K. (2010). An overview of a decade of journal publications about culture and human-computer interaction (HCI). *IFIP Advances in Information and Communication Technology, 316*, 98–112.
10. Danesi, M., & Perron, P. (1999). *Analyzing cultures: An introduction and handbook.* Bloomington: Indiana University Press.
11. de Souza, C. S. (1993). The semiotic engineering of user interface languages. *International Journal of Man-Machine Studies, 39*(5), 753–773.
12. de Souza, C. S. (2005). *The semiotic engineering of human-computer interaction.* Cambridge: The MIT Press.
13. de Souza, C. S. (2012) Semiotics and Human-Computer Interaction. In: Soegaard, Mads and Dam, Rikke Friis. (Org.). Encyclopedia of Human-Computer Interaction. Aarhus: Interaction-Design.Org, 2012, v. 25 - Online at: http://www.interaction-design.org/encyclopedia/semiotics_ and_human-computer_interaction.html. Last visited June, 2012.
14. de Souza, C. S., & Leitão, C. F. (2009). *Semiotic engineering methods for scientific research in HCI.* San Francisco: Morgan and Claypool Publishers.
15. del Gado, E., & Nielsen, J. (1996). *International user interfaces.* New York: Wiley.
16. Dourish, P. (2001). *Where the action is: The foundations of embodied interaction.* Cambridge: The MIT Press.
17. Dourish, P., & Bell, G. (2011). *Divining a digital future: Mess and Mythology in ubiquitous computing.* Cambridge: The MIT Press.
18. Eco, U. (1976). *A theory of semiotics.* Bloomington: Indiana University Press.
19. Fogg, B. J. (2003). *Persuasive technology.* Menlo Park: Morgan Kaufmann.
20. Ford, G., & Gelderbom, H. (2003). The effects of culture on performance achieved through the use of human computer interaction. In *Proceedings of the 2003 annual research conference of the South African institute of computer scientists and information technologists on enablement through technology* (SAICSIT '03). Jarr Eloff, Andries Engelbrecht, Paula Kotz and Mariki Eloff (Eds.). South African Institute for Computer Scientists and Information Technologists, Republic of South Africa, 218–230.
21. Geertz, C. (1973). *The interpretation of cultures: Selected essays.* New York: Basic Books.
22. Geertz, C. (1983). *Local knowledge: Further essays in interpretive anthropology.* New York: Basic Books.
23. Gould, E. W. (2005). Synthesizing the literature on cultural values. In N. Aykin (Ed.), *Usability and internationalization of information technology* (pp. 79–121). Mahwah: Lawrence Erlbaum Associates.
24. Hall, E. T. (1959). *The silent language.* New York: Anchor Books.
25. Hall, E. T. (1966). *The hidden dimension.* New York: Doubleday.
26. Hall, E. T. (1976). *Beyond culture.* New York: Doubleday.
27. Hall, E. T., & Hall, M. R. (1990). *Understanding cultural differences.* Yarmouth: Intercultural Press.
28. Hofstede, G. H. (1984). *Culture's consequences: International differences in work-related values.* London: Sage Publications.
29. Irani, L. C., & Dourish, P. (2009). Postcolonial interculturality. In *Proceedings of the 2009 international workshop on Intercultural collaboration* (IWIC '09). ACM, New York, NY, USA, 249–252.
30. Jakobson, J. R. (1960). Linguistics and poetics. In T. A. Sebeok (Ed.), *Style in language* (pp. 350–377). Cambridge: The MIT Press.
31. Kammersgaard, J. (1988). Four different perspectives on human-computer interaction. *International Journal of Man-Machine Studies, 28*(4), 343–362.
32. Keesing, R. M. (1974). Theories of culture. *Annual Review of Anthropology, 3*, 73–97.
33. Keesing, R. M. (1994). Theories of culture revisited. In R. Borofsky (Ed.), *Assessing cultural anthropology* (pp. 301–310). New York: McGraw-Hill.
34. Kluckhohn, C. (1962). *Culture and behavior: Collected essays.* New York: Free Press of Glencoe.

35. Latour, B. (2009). A cautious prometheus? A few steps toward a philosophy of design (with special attention to Peter Sloterdijk). In Keynote lecture at *Networks of design: Proceedings of the 2008 annual international conference of the design history society* (pp. 2–10). Falmouth: University College Falmouth, Boca Raton: Universal Publishers.

36. Marcus, A. (2002). Global and intercultural user-interface design. In J. Jacko & A. Sears (Eds.), *The human-computer interaction handbook* (pp. 441–463). Mahwah: Lawrence Erlbaum Associates.

37. Muller, M. J., & Kuhn, S. (1993). Participatory design. *Communications of the ACM, 36*(6), 24–28.

38. Nadin, M. (1988). Interface design and evaluation: Semiotic implications. In H. R. Hartson & D. Hix (Eds.), *Advances in human-computer interaction 2* (pp. 45–100). Norwood: Ablex.

39. Nardi, B. A. (1996). *Context and consciousness: Activity theory and human-computer interaction.* Cambridge: The MIT Press.

40. Norman, D. A. (1986). Cognitive engineering. In D. A. Norman & S. W. Draper (Eds.), *User centered systems design* (pp. 31–62). Hillsdale: Laurence Erlbaum.

41. Norman, D. A. (2007). *The design of future things.* New York: Basic Books.

42. Norman, D. A. (2011). *Living with complexity.* Cambridge: The MIT Press.

43. Peirce, C. (1992–1998). *The essential Peirce* (Vols. 1 & 2). Bloomington: Indiana University Press. (Eds. N. Houser & C. Kloesel: The Peirce Edition Project).

44. Sakala, L. (2009). Participatory design in a cross-cultural design context. Master thesis, University of Joensuu. Retrieved March, 2011. In: ftp://www.cs.joensuu.fi/pub/Theses/2009_MSc_Sakala_Lomanzi.pdf.

45. Sangiorgi, U. B. & Barbosa, S. D. J. (2009). MoLIC designer: towards computational support to hci design with MoLIC. In: *Proceedings of the 1st ACM SIGCHI symposium on Engineering interactive computing systems* (EICS '09). ACM, New York, NY, USA, 303–308. DOI=10.1145/1570433.1570489 http://doi.acm.org/10.1145/1570433.1570489.

46. Shen, S., Wooley, M., & Prior, S. (2006). Towards culture-centred design. *Interacting with Computers, 18*(4), 820–852.

47. Tylor, E. B. (2010). *Primitive culture: Researches into the development of mythology, philosophy, religion, art, and custom.* Cambridge: Cambridge University Press.

48. UNESCO. (2011). *The United Nations Educational, Scientific and Cultural Organization.* http://www.unesco.org/new/en/culture/themes/cultural-diversity/ Last visited on December, 2011.

49. Vatrapu, R. (2010). Explaining culture: An outline of a theory of socio-technical interactions. In *Proceedings of the 3rd ACM international conference on intercultural collaboration* (ICIC '10). ACM, New York, NY, USA, 111–120. DOI=10.1145/1841853.1841871 http://doi.acm.org/10.1145/1841853.1841871.

50. Winograd, T., & Flores, F. (1986). *Understanding computers and cognition: A new foundation for design.* Reading: Addison-Wesley.

51. Würtz, E. (2005). A cross-cultural analysis of websites from high-context cultures and low-context cultures. *Journal of Computer-Mediated Communication, 11*(1), article 13. Online at: http://jcmc.indiana.edu/vol11/issue1/wuertz.html.

Chapter 3
Cultural Viewpoint Metaphors

Abstract More than ever before, today one of the challenges for interaction design is the development of systems aiming to attend to the needs and expectations of people with different cultural and social backgrounds. The most widely used perspective in cross-cultural design is internationalization-localization. The result of internationalization and localization is to conceal or neutralize cultural differences among different user communities and contexts of use. We are, however, interested in another situation: one where the design intent is virtually the opposite, to expose and explore cultural diversity. This chapter presents and discusses Cultural Viewpoint Metaphors, an epistemic tool to support the elaboration and evaluation of metacommunicative discourse about cultural diversity.

Cultural Viewpoint Metaphors (CVM) are an epistemic tool intended to inform and to guide interaction design and evaluation whenever explicit communication about (or exploration of) cultural diversity is part of the design intent [13]. The targeted users of CVM are HCI practitioners and researchers. End users of systems elaborated with CVM support will in turn be affected by the way designers interpret and choose to use this conceptual tool.

Inspired by Schön's [14] view about the central role of knowledge in research and design, de Souza [3] argued that, "from a design point of view, epistemic tools contribute to naming and framing design problems, to synthesizing and evaluating solutions, and to elaborating metacommunicative strategies" (ibid., p. 106). Thus, as an epistemic tool, CVM should not be used directly to produce the answer to intercultural problems, but to increase HCI designers' own understanding of the problem, to explore the implications of potential solutions, to generate alternative solutions and to evaluate them against each other.

Unlike other epistemic tools derived from Semiotic Engineering concepts such as the Semiotic Inspection Method (SIM) [4], for instance, the use of CVM in design activities does not depend on prior Semiotic Engineering knowledge. As a typical tool of reflective design, it is intended for designers who want to think over alternatives throughout the design process and to learn in the process.

When dealing with cross-cultural HCI design, the organization of interactive discourse begins with deciding what is the top-level design intent and perspective on culture and intercultural contact. From this decision various choices about cultural content follow, including the kinds of communicative strategies and signification systems that will more effectively and efficiently convey the designer's message.

Usually, when designing for users with widely diverse cultural backgrounds, designers tend to choose between two options: interfaces that aim at minimizing cultural differences and maximizing cultural similarities (one interface *for all*); or interfaces that value cultural differences and provide customized interaction for user groups with distinct values and practices (one interface *for each*). Our work, however, addresses a third alternative, that of deliberately stimulating users to engage in different levels of intercultural contact (when desirable), which may increase their perception about cultural diversity in the particular domain where the system is placed. The next section presents the new perspective brought up by CVM.

3.1   Cultural Viewpoint Metaphors as a Top Level Frame for Cross-Cultural HCI Design

CVM help designers make decisions about possible ways to promote the users' contact with cultural diversity and to communicate such decisions throughout inter-action. The gist of CVM is to lead designers to conceptualize the user as a *traveler* in five different contexts by adopting distinct cultural approximation strategies.

The five distinct perspectives are plotted upon a continuum of cultural approximation which spans from the users' culture, at one end, to a foreign culture, at the other. The adoption of each metaphor entails different cultural mediation rhetoric while building the designer's deputy in human-computer interaction. The continuum of cultural approximation (see Fig. 3.1) shows that at both ends cultural mediation is absent. On the left-side end, *the domestic traveler metaphor* does not expose and explore cultural diversity; instead, it conceals it from the user. Presumably, the designer's intent in this case is not to promote any kind of intercultural contact opportunity for the system's users.

On the right-side end, *the foreigner without translator metaphor* leads users into complete cultural immersion. In this case, the intercultural contact does exist, but with no intermediaries. No explanations or guidance are provided; the users must figure the meaning of foreign culture material on their own.

By choosing one of the remaining metaphors between the two extremes (*the observer at a distance*, *the guided tour visitor*, and *the foreigner with translator metaphors*), designers may communicate cultural diversity with different levels of cultural mediation regarding the foreign culture. The mediated conversation with (and about) the system through the interface language is achieved by interface signs

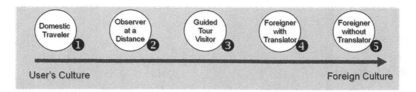

Fig. 3.1 Progressive cultural viewpoint metaphors

intentionally selected by designers to encourage and enable different kinds of inter-cultural contact.

Different organizations of interactive discourse associated with each metaphor (see the next sections) involve the choice of top-level metacommunication styles and structures and the combination of values assigned to two specific cultural variables: language (with values 'native' or 'foreign') and cultural practices (with several domain-dependent values such as 'driving on the left-hand side of the road', 'reading direction from right to left', etc.).

Although 'language' is also a cultural variable, CVM takes 'language' separately. This strategy is also adopted in related work about internationalization [1, 5, 6, 10–12], for instance, where language is usually the first and foremost issue to be dealt with in the design process. It does not mean, however, that other variables could not or should not be considered in isolation in some specific context of cross-cultural design. It only means that, in the context of our research, this segmentation has proved to be simpler and more productive than others.

We represent cultural variables as attribute-value pairs. It should be noted, however, that CVM are not meant to elicit cultural variables, but only to support the design of communication about them. The cultural content that can be used in metacommunication, that is, the linguistic and domain-dependent cultural variables and their values must be elicited with other means. They result from a designer's modeling of the domain and his or her decisions about what type of cultural phenomena must be considered with respect to the tasks supported by the system and the information that goes with them.

Decisions on how to combine the values assigned to language and cultural practices (e.g. presenting the interface in the user's native language, but addressing the user with a foreign degree of formality) and on how much explanation to give about foreign values intentionally selected by the designer can achieve powerful communicative effects.

Figure 3.2 shows how the metaphors are distributed with respect to cultural approximation (horizontal axis) and design levels of cultural mediation and support provided by the metacommunicative discourse (vertical axis). When less help is provided by the designer's deputy, users are more challenged if they find themselves in a foreign cultural setting. Offering more mediation, help and scaffolds, however, corresponds to more laborious design, because the designer's deputy must show and enable foreign cultural practices while attending to the user's native cultural needs. Thus Fig. 3.2 may also be interpreted as a tradeoff guide in cross-cultural design choices.

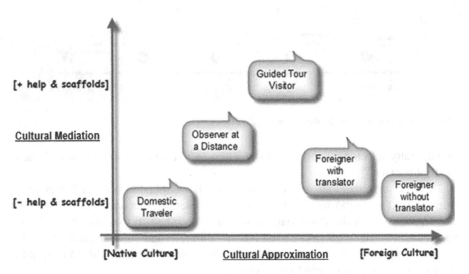

Fig. 3.2 Metaphors' effects while expressing design intent

In the following five sections each conceptual metaphor is presented individually. In order to illustrate their effects on interactive discourse (metacommunication features and cultural variables combination) we use a simple illustrative example from now on. Inspired by previous examples used in Chap. 2, we keep the focus on the culinary domain. The base scenario is about a hypothetical American user, browsing a culinary website which has a stock of international recipes. We show portions of sketched pages collected in existing international websites to illustrate the kinds of effects that can be achieved by designing with each one of the five metaphors. Besides language, the main cultural variables presented in these sketches are: units of measurements, typical ingredients, how and when to prepare and serve meals, and the recipe's origins.

It is worth mentioning that albeit showing interesting cases of metaphors' effects, the sketches we used as illustrations come from existing websites. They have certainly *not been designed with CVM*. We believe that such unintentional observable effects reinforce their epistemic and expressive power. Our choice for proposing metaphors to guide culture-sensitive design is precisely because metaphors are close to our innate and intuitive way of thinking and making sense of the world [8, 9]. As metacommunication happens regardless of the designers' degree of awareness that they are actually communicating [4], the fact that some interface unintentionally communicates cultural content achieving the same effect as one of the proposed metaphors shows how close they are to the way we think about, organize and communicate cultural content in our day-life situations. As remarked by Hunt Jr. [7], "since earliest times, the act of travelling has been seen as a natural metaphor for learning, for the acquisition of experience and knowledge" (ibid., p. 44). Therefore, our sketches

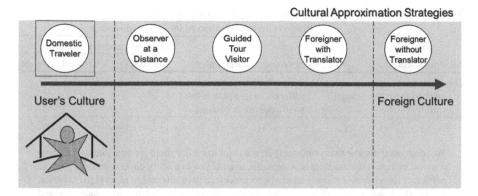

Fig. 3.3 The domestic traveler metaphor

illustrate intuitive and unconscious metaphorical reasoning about intercultural contacts in HCI using the basic 'journey' metaphor.

3.1.1   The Domestic Traveler Metaphor

The domestic traveler metaphor's intended effect on the expression of design is that of cultural isolation. Therefore, by design, users are located in their native culture, without being explicitly exposed to foreign culture's signs. As a result, in the specific context where designers supposedly want to promote targeted users' contact with cultural diversity, using the domestic traveler metaphor achieves the opposite of what is intended (see Fig. 3.3). However, the metaphor is useful if there are portions of the system in which, for the users' safety for instance, this is desired (e.g. using familiar, rather than unfamiliar, credit card processing steps in online commercial activities).

Design guided by *the domestic traveler metaphor*, then, typically isolates users from explicit intercultural contacts and conceals the presence of elements coming from another culture. Metacommunication features should deemphasize cultural differences and make the user's culture dominate. Regarding design decisions about the two cultural variables, both language and cultural practices should come from users' culture. In other words, designers should use the users' native language and encode the users' own cultural practice (see Table 3.1) when elaborating metacommunicative discourse about cultural diversity.

The top-level metacommunication message, based on the Semiotic Engineering metacommunication template (see Chap. 2, Sect. 2.1), and guided by *the domestic traveler metaphor*, will include the following elements, among others:

Table 3.1 The domestic traveler metaphor effects on metacommunication

| | Effects on the organization of interactive discourse | | |
| | | Cultural variables | |
Metaphor expression	Metacommunication features	Language	Cultural practice
Domestic traveler. No markers from the foreign culture.	Design neutralizes cultural differences and makes the user's culture dominate.	User's	User's

> We [designers] assume that you [users] do not want to bother about foreign country information and culture while using this system. So, even if you explicitly choose or use a specific portion of the system that involves elements produced in or referenced to foreign countries, the interface will systematically communicate with you using your native language and alluding to your cultural practices.

To illustrate the use of ***the domestic traveler metaphor*** in our hypothetical culinary website scenario, think of recipes coming from various cultures and being presented as if they were local recipes (i.e., American dish recipes, since our hypothesized user is American). The interface language and cultural culinary practices are referenced to the United States, even if users choose recipes from foreign countries. Traces of this metaphor have been found in real websites such as Recipe.com website[1] (see corresponding sketch in Fig. 3.4).

As seen in Fig. 3.4, the illustrated website allows users to find international recipes. However, they are presented as American recipes (see the ingredients, directions, units of measurement and so on) and there are no explicit references to the Swiss *culture* (except perhaps for the names of cheeses, which are however customarily used in North American culture). Although 'Cheese Fondue' is a classic Swiss dish, the website does not take this as an opportunity to explore Swiss cultural practices or provide information about Switzerland (e.g. a link to Swiss cuisine in Wikipedia).

3.1.2   The Observer at a Distance Metaphor

The observer at a distance metaphor's intended effect on the expression of design is that of a gentle and distant contact with different cultural contexts. The concept behind this metaphor is that the cultural markers[2] [2] of the foreign culture are

---

[1] http://www.recipe.com (as in February 2012).

[2] According to Wendy Barber and Albert Badre, cultural markers are: "the detailed list of cultural markers corresponding to web design elements contains color, spatial organization, fonts, shapes, icons, metaphors, geography, language, flags, sounds, motion, preferences for text versus graphics, directionality of how language is written, help features and navigation tools." [2, p.1]

Fig. 3.4 Recipe.com website (Cheese Fondue recipe)

presented to the targeted user as 'information', not as 'experience' (see Fig. 3.5). The designer exposes the user to other culture providing some intermediate levels of cultural mediation (see Fig. 3.2). In other words, the user hears about facts pertaining to the foreign culture, but does not engage in foreign cultural practices.

With this metaphor, the users' native culture dominates the design, but the designers give hints about the foreign culture. Metacommunication features only include references to it among dominant signs selected from the targeted users' native culture (see Table 3.2).

Regarding design decisions about the two cultural variables, both language and cultural practices should come from the users' culture. Interface elements that refer to cultural practices (cultural markers) are selected in the user's culture and a narrative (or description) of contrastive foreign culture features is provided.

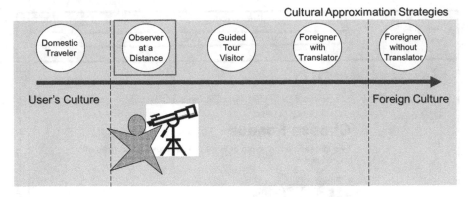

Fig. 3.5 The observer at a distance metaphor

Table 3.2 The observer at a distance metaphor effects on metacommunication

	Effects on the organization of interactive discourse		
		Cultural variables	
Metaphor expression	Metacommunication features	Language	Cultural practice
Observer at a distance. The cultural markers of another culture are communicated as 'information' (not as an experience the user can 'feel').	Interface elements which represent cultural practices are presented according to the user's culture. Narrative about the foreign culture provides factual information about what is different from one's own culture.	User's	User's

The top-level metacommunication message using *the observer at a distance metaphor* will include the following elements, among others:

> We [designers] assume that you [users] may be interested in learning more about foreign countries and cultures. So, the system shows several markers of contrastive foreign features, presented to you as bits of information. However, the interface will systematically communicate with you using your language and your native cultural practices.

Following our hypothetical culinary scenario, if an American user is browsing a website designed according to *the observer at a distance metaphor* and chooses to see a recipe from a foreign country, he will find cultural hints about this country's cultural practices. Some cultural practices such as the selection of ingredients, use of units of measurement, and style of instructions are instantiated with reference to the user's own culture (American). However, the user is invited to 'learn more' if he or she wishes to do it.

The Global Gourmet website[3] (see corresponding sketch in Fig. 3.6) illustrates the kinds of effects that can be achieved with *the observer at a distance metaphor*.

---

[3] http://www.globalgourmet.com/ (as in February 2012).

Fig. 3.6 Global Gourmet website (global destinations)

The section title ('Global Destinations') and respective image 'The world on a plate' sign invite users to search recipes from foreign countries. The country's names are linked to at least one recipe from that particular country, presented along with bits of information about regional traditions in the country's cuisine (such as foreign influences) and so on (see Fig. 3.7).

If the user chooses Austria as destination, for instance, information snippets about the country are shown. For example, the user can learn about historical and modern culinary influences, traditional recipes, size of the country and its population. All is presented in the users' language (English) but the original recipes' names are also shown in German, next to the English translation (see Fig. 3.7).

Selected recipes from Austria are presented in English, and so are the ingredients and units of measurements from North American culture. The Austrian flag link signifies the presence of a foreign culture and invites users to 'learn more' (see Fig. 3.8), but there are no contrastive interpretations of American and Austrian cultures.

Fig. 3.7 Global Gourmet website (destination: Austria)

Cross-cultural design guided by ***the observer at a distance metaphor*** allows us to attend to users that are only marginally interested in intercultural exposure. Assuming that they will occasionally be inclined to learn a few new facts about a foreign culture, the designers can put in place a number of mechanisms to support the users' occasional browsing.

3.1.3   The Guided Tour Visitor Metaphor

The guided tour visitor metaphor (see Fig. 3.9) presents the foreign culture through interface signs and interaction forms borrowed from this culture's practices. Cultural markers of another culture appear to the user as 'illustration' (e.g., a typical foreign ingredient is present, but a similar local one is also suggested). The metaphor's

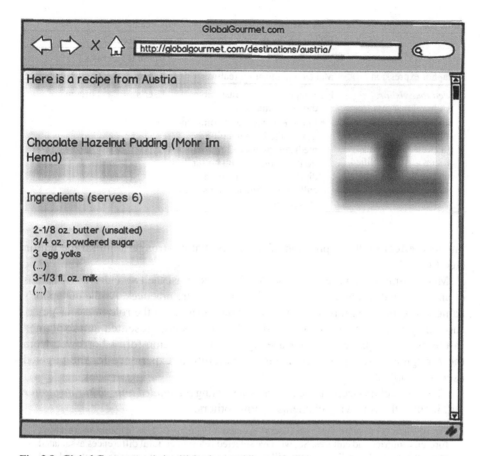

Fig. 3.8 Global Gourmet website (chocolate pudding recipe)

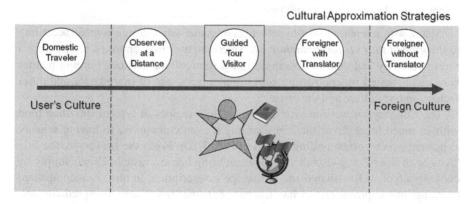

Fig. 3.9 The guided tour visitor metaphor

Table 3.3 The guided tour visitor metaphor effects on metacommunication

	Effects on the organization of interactive discourse		
		Cultural variables	
Metaphor expression	Metacommunication features	Language	Cultural practice
Guided tour visitor. Cultural markers from another culture are 'illustrated' to the user (aspects of cultural issues are exemplified and explained in the user's language).	Design provides contrast between the two cultures. An interpreted view and commentary on the foreign culture mediates the user's approximation and contact with cultural diversity. The user's own culture is dominant and serves as reference.	User's	Foreign

intended effect on the expression of design is that of stronger cultural mediation (see Fig. 3.2).

Metacommunication features should ideally contrast the two cultures by means of an interpretation and commentary of foreign culture practices. As the metaphor's name suggests, using this metaphor places the designer in the role of a tour guide, showing a new place to visitors. Cultural variables are presented and explained in the user's language, but interface signs and interaction forms borrowed from the foreign culture's practices intensify intercultural experience for the targeted user (see Table 3.3).

The top-level metacommunication message using *the guided tour visitor metaphor* will include the following elements, among others:

> We [designers] assume that you [users] are actively interested in learning more about foreign countries and cultures. So, we have selected relevant cultural differences associated to what you are doing. The system will give you the opportunity to engage in intercultural contact if you follow the guidance provided. The interface will systematically communicate with you in your native language, but it will let you choose between foreign or native cultural practices and give you useful explanations.

Again, with reference to our hypothetical scenario, when design is made according to *the guided tour visitor metaphor*, an American user may choose a recipe from a foreign country and then engage in designed intercultural contact. Foreign recipes may be presented by contrasting cooking practices, use of ingredients and other factors, in one culture and the other.

The Culinary.net website,[4] for instance, offers recipes of typical Brazilian food with so much local *flavor* that the user might even come close to having sensory experience (see corresponding sketch in Fig. 3.10). From the first page, the title "A taste of Brazil" suggests that anyone can bring home a taste of Brazil simply by cooking a typical Brazilian dish. The recipe's description, in turn, is accompanied by an inviting explanation of what 'Cachaça & Lime Parfait' and its ingredients are,

---

[4] http://www.culinary.net (as in February 2012).

Fig. 3.10 Culinary.net website (articles)

of how to pronounce their Brazilian names, and what alternative American ingredients can substitute for Brazilian ingredients (see Fig. 3.11).

The Just Brazil website,[5] in turn, presents typical Brazilian food with its original names (see corresponding sketch in Fig. 3.12) and shows the ingredients with the units of measurement of both the American and Brazilian cultures (see Fig. 3.13). The website also presents images of the most popular dishes with detailed explanations.

The Sonia Portuguese website[6] is yet another good example of how this metaphor may have been intuitively used (see corresponding sketch in Fig. 3.14). The Brazilian colors (green and yellow) and images of typical Brazilian scenes give us the idea of how it is to be in this country. The recipes' names and ingredients are presented in two languages (Portuguese and English). The user is thus immediately

---

[5] www.justbrazil.org/brazil/recipes/ (as accessed in February 2012).

[6] www.Sonia-portuguese.com (as accessed in February of 2012).

Fig. 3.11 Culinary.net website (Parfait recipe)

in contact with foreign units of measurement contrasting with the ones used in his or her native culture.

Designing purposefully with **the guided tour visitor metaphor** in mind allows designers to present, explain, and enable contact with cultural diversity in a much more explicit way. Instead of just providing information about cultural features (as **the observer at a distance metaphor** does), designers may go into demonstrating what these features are. The idea is to elaborate metacommunication that motivates users to feel some of the impact of finding themselves in the context of a foreign culture.

3.1.4   The Foreigner with Translator Metaphor

The foreigner with translator metaphor (see Fig. 3.15) allows users to sense what it is like to be immersed in a foreign culture. The only scaffold provided for the

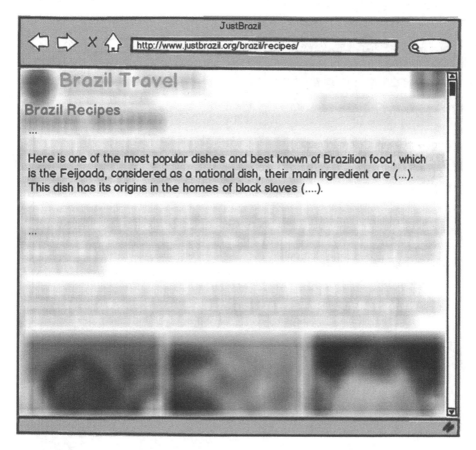

Fig. 3.12 Just Brazil website (recipes)

experience is a translation of linguistic material into the users' native language. When designing by ***the foreigner with translator metaphor***, designers intend to provide weak cultural mediation (see Fig. 3.2).

Cultural markers are presented directly, without introduction or explanation, in the same way as they are shown to users that are native in that culture. The result of designing guided by ***the foreigner with translator metaphor*** is that the designer does not provide additional support to international users, except of linguistic translation. Cultural practices will be exposed to "foreigners" in the same way as to "natives". Consequently, users can directly experience foreign cultural practices, but they will still be able to use their native language in interaction with the system (see Table 3.4).

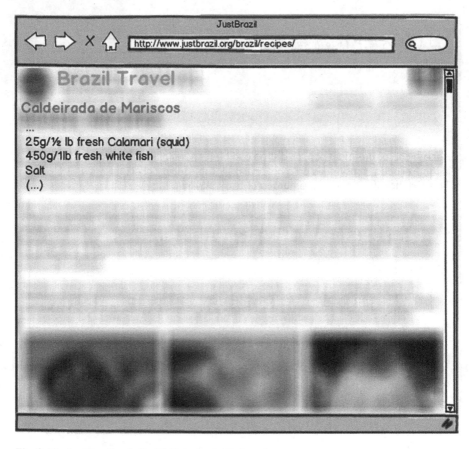

Fig. 3.13 Just Brazil website (Caldeirada de Mariscos)

The top-level metacommunication message using *the foreigner with translator metaphor* will include the following elements:

> We [designers] assume that you [users] want to get in touch with foreign countries and cultures. So, the system will expose you to the same cultural markers and practices as native users from the foreign culture are exposed to. And although the system will always communicate with you in your native language, it will not give you explanations and further information to help you navigate the culture. You will be able to figure it all out for yourself.

Keeping with the same example as in previous illustrations, using *the foreigner with translator metaphor* means that recipes from foreign cultures are only translated into the users' native language. Everything else refers directly to the foreign culture. Such is the case of Brazilian Recipes website,[7] for example, where many Brazilian recipes are presented in English, in the same way as recipes are presented

---

[7] http://brazilianrecipes.org/brazilian_food/ (as accessed in February 2012).

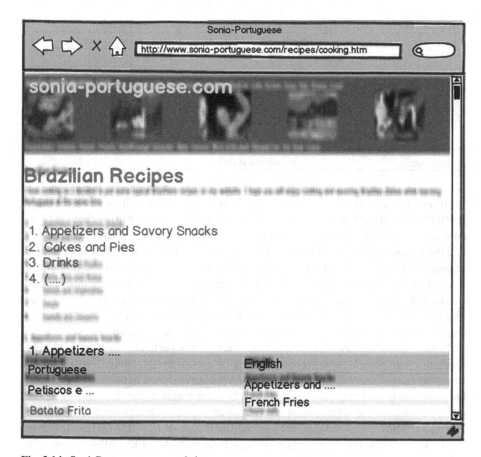

Fig. 3.14 SoniaPortuguese.com website

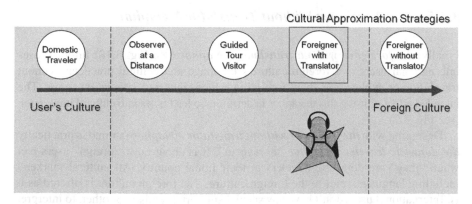

Fig. 3.15 The foreigner with translator metaphor

Table 3.4 The foreigner with translator metaphor effects on metacommunication

	Effects on the organization of interactive discourse		
		Cultural variables	
Metaphor expression	Metacommunication features	Language	Cultural practice
Foreigner with translator. Cultural markers of another culture can be directly 'experienced' by the user, although in the user's own language.	Communication content is presented in the same way as it is presented to native users from the foreign culture. Only a linguistic translation is done.	User's	Foreign

to Brazilian users. There aren't any adaptations, explanations, illustrations or other scaffolds to help foreign users make sense of some culturally sensitive elements (see corresponding sketches in Figs. 3.16 and 3.17). In Fig. 3.17, in particular, we see that the recipe tells the user to use "1 pack of tapioca starch". For a typical Brazilian, talking about packs of tapioca starch helps them sense immediately the amount of starch to be used in the recipe (the "450 g" in parentheses is subsidiary information for users that have stocked tapioca in some other container than *a pack*). We can see that the website privileges Brazilian users, and provides minimal scaffolds for international users who want to venture into the world of Brazilian cuisine.

Notice that there are clear indications that in this particular context using *the foreigner with translator metaphor* may not be a good design choice. Nevertheless, a number of international websites on the Internet are designed in this way, presenting the same sort of challenges for foreign users. In some domains, however, this metaphor makes perfect sense. Portions of international search websites such as Google's Advanced Search, for example, are a good illustration of how this metaphor can be used successfully. The same applies to technical websites, like online support for software products or electronic equipment.

3.1.5 The Foreigner Without Translator Metaphor

Finally, *the foreigner without translator metaphor* (see Fig. 3.18) fully exposes international users to a foreign culture's language and cultural practices, without translation or explanation about foreign interface signs and interaction forms. The intended effect of using this metaphor in design is to lead users into cultural immersion (see Fig. 3.2).

Designing with *the foreigner without translator metaphor* in mind is practically *the domestic traveler metaphor* "in reverse". It is about how "foreign" users feel when "they" are domestic travelers in their home country. All cultural markers, including language, refer to the foreign culture. The foreign culture is offered as it is. International users don't have any special support, linguistic or other, to interpret interface signs and interaction forms that have been designed for natives of a foreign culture (see Table 3.5).

Fig. 3.16 Brazilian recipes website

The top-level metacommunication message using ***the foreigner without translator
metaphor*** will include the following elements, among others:

We [designers] assume that you [users] want to put yourselves in foreign shoes, and to
experience how it feels to be in foreign countries and cultures. So, the system will expose
you to the same cultural markers and practices as native users from the foreign culture are
exposed to. Once interacting with the system you will be treated as one of them. The system
will communicate with you using language and cultural practices that are not native to you,
and it will not give you translations, explanations and further information to help you navigate
the culture. You will be able to figure it all out for yourself.

In the hypothetical scenario used in all the illustrations for preceding metaphors,
recipes would be presented without any linguistic translation, explanation or cultural
adaptation. The Online Recipe Guide website,[8] for instance, is an international

---

[8] www.onlinerecipeguide.com (as accessed in February 2012).

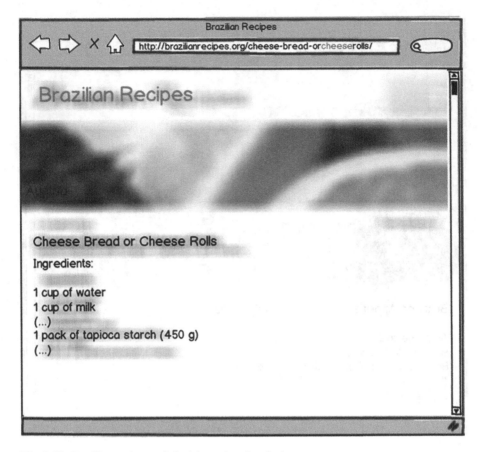

Fig. 3.17 Brazilian recipes website (cheese bread recipe)

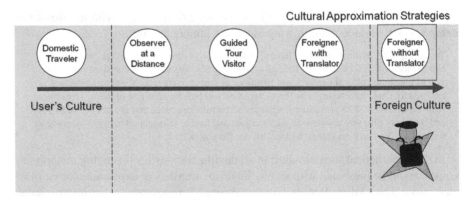

Fig. 3.18 The foreigner without translator metaphor

Table 3.5 The foreigner without translator metaphor effects on metacommunication

	Effects on the organization of interactive discourse		
		Cultural variables	
Metaphor expression	Metacommunication features	Language	Cultural practice
Foreigner without translator. Users are treated as natives from a foreign culture.	The culture of others is offered as it is.	Foreign	Foreign

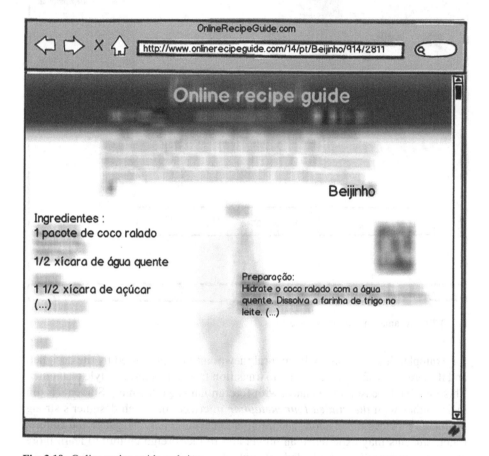

Fig. 3.19 Online recipe guide website

website (see corresponding sketch in Fig. 3.19) in which Brazilian recipes are available to users from all over the world. Thus, the Brazilian recipes are presented in Portuguese, even if the user chooses one of the other available language preferences in the website. Only images can help an American user, for instance, realize what "Beijinho" is, a popular sweet enjoyed at Brazilian birthday parties.

Although designing with *the foreigner without translator metaphor* in mind may at first seem like a mistaken design choice, there are certain advantages in it if,

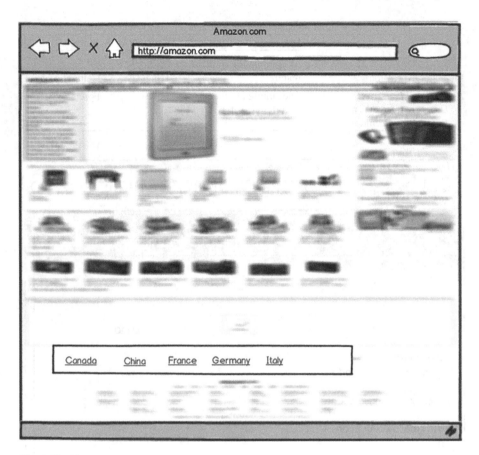

Fig. 3.20 The amazon.com home page

for example, this is not the only cultural viewpoint metaphor used by the designer, and if there are clearly marked ways to transition from one interface style to another. This may be the case, for instance, with foreign language learning. Students begin their studies with *the guided tour metaphor* interface, in which designer's strong mediation provides explanations and information about foreign language and culture. Later, students may experience an immersion in the foreign culture to learn more about the language in real full-fledged context of use.

Cross-cultural systems interfaces may actually be designed using more than one of the proposed metaphors. As already mentioned, it may be desirable to adopt cultural isolation for certain tasks and activities supported by the system (e.g. credit card payment in e-commerce applications), but to intentionally expose the user to experiencing various degrees of foreignness in others (e.g. freight and delivery options for merchandise that is going to be purchased in one country and received in another). In other words, with applications involving commercial transactions, the interface for payment tasks may be best designed following *the domestic traveler*

Table 3.6 Cultural viewpoint metaphors

Metaphor expression	Effects on the organization of interactive discourse	Cultural variables	
	Metacommunication features	Language	Cultural practice
Domestic traveler. No markers from the foreign culture.	Design neutralizes cultural differences and makes the user's culture dominate.	User's	User's
Observer at a distance. The cultural markers of another culture are communicated as 'information' (not as an experience the user can 'feel').	Interface elements which represent cultural practices are presented according to the user's culture. Narrative about the foreign culture provides factual information about what is different from one's own culture.	User's	User's
Guided tour visitor. Cultural markers from another culture are 'illustrated' to the user (aspects of cultural issues are exemplified and explained in the user's language).	Design provides contrast between the two cultures. An interpreted view and commentary on the foreign culture mediates the user's approximation and contact with cultural diversity. The user's own culture is dominant and serves as reference.	User's	Foreign
Foreigner with translator. Cultural markers of another culture can be directly 'experienced' by the user, although in the user's own language.	Communication content is presented in the same way as it is presented to native users from the foreign culture. Only a linguistic translation is done.	User's	Foreign
Foreigner without translator. Users are treated as natives from a foreign culture.	The culture of others is offered as it is.	Foreign	Foreign

metaphor to avoid misunderstandings in transactions involving money. However, users might benefit from knowing that, for example, unlike what happens in their native country, in the foreign country where the purchased goods are going to be delivered, the receiver does not get the goods at home. He or she has to go to a specifically designated location and redeem the goods, thanks to frequent cases of imported goods being stolen from delivery trucks on the road (or whatever other reason). Whether the communication of such relevant content is going to be expressed through *the observer at a distance*, *the guided tour visitor*, *the foreigner with translator* or *the foreigner without translator metaphor* is a design choice.

Designing systems with only one dominant metaphor is also possible. For instance, the amazon.com website can be used by people from all cultures. But for foreigners that have never lived in North America, the experience is that of a *foreigner without translator*. For example, although rebates on electronic equipment prices are boldly advertised on their home page, such rebates are actually not valid for users importing equipment into some other countries. This information is not conveyed up front, and in the absence of mediation it may go unnoticed well into the purchasing process, when the user finally indicates where the item is to be delivered. Links to international sites at the bottom of the page (see corresponding sketch in Fig. 3.20) lead to similarly designed websites, where residents of the website's owner's country are domestic users and customers from other countries feel like foreigners without translator.

In conclusion to this chapter, we should remark that the instantiation of portions of metacommunication messages presented here shows that designers can clearly achieve very different rhetorical effects with mediation by choosing this or that cultural viewpoint metaphor. From cultural isolation at one end to total cultural immersion at the other, the metaphors not only represent progressive cultural approximation landmarks, but they also suggest that some are better than the others if designers want to be more helpful and informative, or the other way around.

So far we have illustrated and explained the effect of our proposed viewpoint metaphors in design (see Table 3.6). The next chapter describes and presents results of a two-step case study carried out to assess the potential of CVM in designing and evaluating intercultural experience.

References

1. Aykin, N. (2005). *Usability and internationalization of information technology*. Mahwah: Lawrence Erlbaum.
2. Barber, W., & Badre, A. (1998, June 5). Culturability: The merging of culture and usability. In *Proceedings of the 4th conference on human factors & the web*. Basking Ridge: Online publication. Available at http://www.research.att.com/conf/hfweb/proceedings/barber/index.htm. Last visited in January, 2012.

3. de Souza, C. S. (2005). *The semiotic engineering of human-computer interaction*. Cambridge: The MIT Press.
4. de Souza, C. S., & Leitão, C. F. (2009). *Semiotic engineering methods for scientific research in HCI*. San Francisco: Morgan and Claypool Publishers.
5. Del Gado, E., & Nielsen, J. (1996). *International user interfaces*. New York: Wiley.
6. Fernandes, T. (1995). *Global interface design: A guide to designing international user interfaces*. San Diego: Academic Press Professional.
7. Hunt, B. C., Jr. (1976). Travel metaphors and the problem of knowledge. *Modern Language Studies, 6*(1), 44–47. Online at: http://www.jstor.org/stable/3194392. Last visited on February, 2012.
8. Lakoff, G. (1993). The contemporary theory of metaphor. In A. Ortony (Ed.), *Metaphor and thought* (2nd ed., pp. 202–251). Cambridge: Cambridge University Press.
9. Lakoff, G., & Johnson, M. (1980). *Metaphors we live by*. Chicago: University of Chicago Press.
10. Marcus, A. (2001). International and intercultural user interfaces. In C. Stephanidis (Ed.), *User interfaces for all: Concepts, methods, and tool* (pp. 47–63). Mahwah: Lawrence Erlbaum.
11. Nielsen, J. (1990). Usability testing of international interfaces. In J. Nielsen (Ed.), *Designing user interfaces for international use*. New York: Elsevier.
12. Russo, P., & Boor, S. (1993). How fluent is your interface?: designing for international users. In *Proceedings of the INTERACT '93 and CHI '93 conference on human factors in computing systems*, (CHI '93). ACM, New York, NY, USA, 342–347.
13. Salgado, L. C. C., Souza, C. S., & Leitao, C. F. (2009). Conceptual Metaphors for Designing Multi-cultural Applications. In: *Web Congress, 2009. LA-WEB '09. Latin American*, vol., no., pp.105–111, 9–11 Nov. 2009. doi: 10.1109/LA-WEB.2009.17.
14. Schön, D. (1983). *The reflective practitioner: How professionals think in action*. New York: Basic Books.

Chapter 4
A Case Study: Re-designing the AVIS Website

Abstract This chapter presents and discusses the main results of a case study carried out to assess HCI designers' and evaluators' understanding and use of CVM, as well as the metaphors' potential for informing and improving the design and evaluation of cross-cultural systems. In this case study, our research question was: how can CVM support HCI practitioners (if at all) at design and evaluation time? The two-step case study used the AVIS website both in (re)design and evaluation time. Our conclusion is that CVM indeed contribute to HCI research in cross-cultural design, since they frame, organize and structure HCI designers' thinking and thus function as an epistemic tool to support the elaboration of culture-sensitive meta-communication discourse.

In order to find out *how (if at all)* **Cultural Viewpoint Metaphors (CVM)** *can support HCI professionals/practitioners at design and evaluation time* we ran two different experiments which contributed to a broader case study (see Fig. 4.1) with the AVIS website.[1] One of them assessed how CVM can be used at design time (Step One) and the other assessed how CVM can be used at evaluation time (Step Two). We kept a practical perspective in both experiments – the types of tasks proposed to participants are familiar to any professional working in HCI design and evaluation. With findings from both steps we refined aspects of the overall CVM approach and generated further research topics for future work.

For Step One (CVM at design time), we recruited six participants and asked them to do a re-design activity. They should meet the following recruiting criteria: to have a non-American cultural background (the Avis website is guided by American culture); to have good knowledge of HCI design; and to have reading

---

[1] www.avis.com

L.C.C. Salgado et al., *A Journey Through Cultures: Metaphors for Guiding the Design of Cross-Cultural Interactive Systems*, Human–Computer Interaction Series, DOI 10.1007/978-1-4471-4114-3_4, © Springer-Verlag London 2013

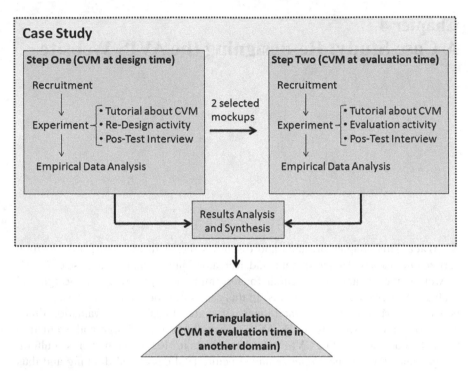

Fig. 4.1 Research steps

fluency in English. Participants should also have different cultural background from one another. Re-design alternatives elaborated by people with different cultural backgrounds could be expected to contrast with the American cultural features displayed in the Avis website and thus give us valuable input for research.

The experiment scenario asked participants to design for a typical American AVIS customer who is about to make a rental car reservation and chooses a foreign location for pick-up. This location is culturally familiar to the participants (and varies from one participant to the other, according to their specific cultural backgrounds). In other words, the targeted user *is not* somebody with the same cultural background as the participants', but participants are at ease with the foreign culture that this user will deal with in the process of renting (and driving) a car abroad.

In different individual sessions, the six participants listened to a tutorial on CVM (including concepts and examples) and then generated re-design alternatives (mockups) for the AVIS website using CVM as a guide. When finished, they answered questions about the experiment in a brief individual interview.

Two mockups produced by this group of six were selected for the second experiment (Step Two), which involved four participants. These should have good experience in HCI evaluation and reading fluency in English. Unlike in the first experiment, in the second one the participants' cultural background was not a recruitment criterion, since the focus was now on tracing the presence of CVM in design. This was an interesting opportunity to explore how different individuals elaborate meanings associated to the various metaphors.

The four participants listened to a tutorial introducing CVM (including concepts and examples) and then inspected a set of mockups following the proposed scenario for this experiment. They were asked to use CVM as a guide in the activity. As with the previous group, we also made a brief individual post-test interview with participants about the experiment.

We should mention that the level of knowledge in Semiotic Engineering was *not* a factor for recruiting participants in either of the experiments. We wished to assess what CVM meant and how they were used by participants regardless of their preference for one HCI approach or another.

We used non-predictive interpretive methods typical of qualitative investigation [2, 6] throughout the whole case study. This methodology is especially fit for studies like ours, which aim at exploring intensively and at greater depth a specific research question. We thus worked with a small group of participants, focusing on the identification of meanings and interpretation thereof. By identifying various meanings that the participants assigned to CVM, we could investigate how they elaborated and used them to design and to evaluate metacommunication discourse.

The primary empirical evidence in this research was the *participants' discourse*. In Step One, we collected discourse about the mockups and the re-design activity. In Step Two we collected evidence about the evaluation process and its results. In both steps we collected the participants' impressions and opinions expressed during post-test interviews.

As secondary empirical evidence, we also analyzed the mockups (from Step One) and the evaluation reports (from Step Two). We examined how consistent the evidence was in comparison with CVM concepts and built a semiotic reference for primary evidence analysis (i.e. a collection of articulated interface-related signs to compare with the participants' verbal statements in discourse). Specifically in the semiotic analysis of mockups we identified how participants represented cultural variables through interface signs, as well as the kinds of signs (texts, videos, images, graphs and so on) and interaction styles (contrasts, simulation, tips) that they chose.

Our aim in steps One and Two was not to analyze the quality of the final product of design and evaluation (mockups and evaluation reports, respectively). Such products depend more heavily on the participants' technical abilities and talent than on the interpretive processes and reflections that constituted the focus of our interest.

The participants' discourse produced in each step was analyzed separately, using discourse analysis techniques [8]. We carried out a systematic exploration of discourse material in order to find out major meaning categories in it. This exploration began with an intra-participant analysis, which identifies meaning categories in the material produced by *each* participant. Then we proceeded to an inter-participant analysis, which identifies meaning categories recurring across *multiple* participant discourse. Finally, we drew our conclusions based on the set of categorized meanings that guide the interpretation of findings and help us answer the primary research question.

The triangulation that serves as scientific validation in qualitative research [2, 6, 15] was achieved with an experiment using CVM to evaluate cross-cultural HCI design in a different domain (namely, the FIFA website featuring events of the 2010 World Cup in South Africa).

According to Denzin & Lincoln [6], triangulation in qualitative research challenges interpretation achieved in specific situations with knowledge generated in a substantially different situation. Different perspectives of the same object, explored in different contexts, give plausibility and consistency to the interpretation process, promoting more in-depth understanding of the phenomenon in question. Thus, we compared and contrasted final results from our Case Study (overall results from Steps One and Two with AVIS) with findings from the experiment with FIFA, looking once more for consistency and congruence. Section 1.4 presents the process and product of this case study's triangulation.

Most of the participants in our experiments are Brazilian and Portuguese is their mother tongue. Therefore, collected discourse evidence has been mainly produced in Portuguese. In the presentation that follows, we have translated Portuguese material into English.[2] Grammar and style mistakes made by participants in the original speech have not been corrected in the translation, unless they compromised the understanding of the speaker's discourse when taken out of its original context.

Before we begin to present the details of the case study, it is useful to have some information about Avis. AVIS Rent a car System, LCC and its subsidiaries operate "one of the world's best-known car rental brands with approximately 5,100 locations in more than 165 countries".[3] Avis has a USA-based Global website with more than 50 localized versions for countries around the world. They have customized interfaces for each particular audience, like the USA (http://www.avis.com), Israel (http://www.avis.co.il/) and China (http://www.avischina.com/), for instance. In all of them, customers (users) can make, view, modify and cancel car rental reservations. Some of the websites also offer convenience services, such as vehicle delivery coordinated with flight destinations, chauffer drives, etc. We focus, however, on a very specific task, namely "making a rental car reservation" (see the task model in Fig. 4.2).

4.1 Step One: Cultural Viewpoint Metaphors at Design Time

The purpose of this step was to analyze the designers' understanding and use of CVM in a re-design activity, as well as the metaphors' potential for informing and improving the design of cross-cultural applications. We worked with six HCI designers who had good knowledge level in HCI, reading fluency in English and different intercultural experience among them. They had different nationalities and/ or had lived in different foreign countries (see Table 4.1).

Four of the six experiment sessions (P1.1, P1.3, P1.4 and P1.5) were run at the Department of Informatics at PUC-Rio, with duration of approximately 2 h. The other

---

[2] Original transcriptions are listed in [12].
[3] Extracted from http://www.avis.com/ (as in February, 2012).

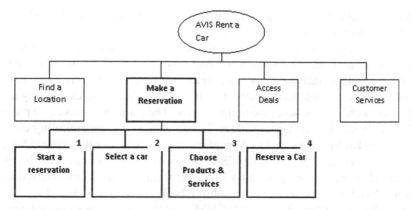

Fig. 4.2 The structure of the task model for making a car reservation in the AVIS website

Table 4.1 Participants' cultural background and corresponding targeted user

Id	Nationality	Participants' cultural background explored in the experiment scenario	Targeted user: an American residing in the USA who chooses…
P1.1	Brazilian	Studying and working in England for 18 months	City in the UK for the car pick-up.
P1.2	Mexican	Living in Mexico	City in Mexico for the car pick-up.
P1.3	Brazilian and Israeli	Studying and working in Israel for 6 years, but living in Brazil.	City in Israel for the car pick-up.
P1.4	Brazilian	Living in Brazil	City in Brazil for the car pick-up.
P1.5	Brazilian	Studying and working in Montreal, Canada (Québec) for 6 years.	City in Canadian French Province for the car pick-up.
P1.6	Brazilian	Studying and working in Toronto, Canada (Ontario) for 3 years	City in Canadian British Province for the car pick-up.

two sessions (P1.2 and P1.6) were run remotely, with video-conference support. All sessions included the following sequential activities:

1. The researcher presented the experiment goals and collected the participants' consent.
2. The participant filled out a questionnaire giving detailed information about his or her experience abroad, as well as his or her experience with HCI design.
3. The researcher presented a tutorial introducing CVM in tutorial.
4. The participant examined the AVIS website and generated re-design alternatives for it following a specific scenario of use and requirements (see below).
5. The researcher carried out a post-test interview with the participant.

   The post-test interview aimed at collecting discourse evidence regarding the designers' perceptions, comments and explanations about: (i) their design alternatives; (ii) the design process, i.e., how the proposed metaphors affected (or not) their thinking over the interaction design; (iii) what they found easy or difficult to do; and, (iv) what they learned with the experiment.

The scenario used for this experiment placed the participant in the role of someone who works in a project to re-design the AVIS website. AVIS supposedly wants to minimize problems that their customers have been facing when they rent cars in foreign countries. Problems typically stem from cultural differences that play a role when using a car abroad, hence the re-design goal. The participant's task is to propose re-design alternatives to improve intercultural contact by communicating cultural diversity guided by the cultural viewpoint metaphors. The user they should have in mind is an American, residing in the USA, who makes a car reservation on the AVIS website and chooses a foreign country location for car pick-up. The location in each session depended on the participant's cultural background (see Table 4.1).

As explained in Chap. 3 (Sect. 3.1) CVM are not meant to elicit cultural content and variables, but only to guide the design of communication about it. The cultural content to be used in metacommunication, that is, the linguistic and domain-dependent cultural variables, with their corresponding values, must elicited using other tools and methods (like ethnographic studies, for instance). Thus, participants received a cultural information checklist with pre-fetched *cultural variables* (but not their values, which participants were supposed to know, given their background and personal history). These variables should be considered regarding task-related interaction and information presented by the re-designed system. The list included variables such as the minimum legal age to drive, units of measurement, the cultural meaning of 'near' and 'far', the meaning of car categories (like "economy car"), road conventions, etc. Choosing which variables and values should be used (or not) in re-design was part of the participants' task.

Although participants were invited to represent their solutions through handmade mockups,[4] P1.3 and P1.5 decided to represent theirs in the form of a "to do list", which merged design principles and requirements that they should verify in their design. All participants were introduced to the whole set of five metaphors in the tutorial, but we encouraged them to use only the ones where explicit intercultural mediation is expressed (*the observer at a distance*, *the guided tour visitor* and *the foreigner with translator metaphor*). Each individual was asked to produce three re-design alternatives. The purpose of this specific requirement was to verify how the CVM helped designers (if at all) to explore different levels of progressive cultural approximation (see Chap. 3 – Sect. 3.1, p. 44).

4.1.1 Detailed Results

In Step One, the main categories of analysis emerging from our interpretation are: (i) difficulties in understanding CVM; (ii) evidence of the epistemic nature of CVM; and (iii) evidence that CVM help designers to communicate cultural diversity.

---

[4] The whole set of participants' mockups is available in [12].

Category (i) is more practical than the other two and helped us to improve CVM description, the names and examples for each metaphor. Categories (ii) and (iii), in turn, helped us with more scientific and theoretical explorations.

4.1.1.1 Difficulties in Understanding CVM

In the process of learning a new concept, doubts and misunderstandings always occur. Therefore, our analysis focused on items that are not just a matter of first-time-encounter blunders. Specifically, we found evidence of difficulties with CVM due to unclear definitions of metaphors and the cultural approximation continuum. *The guided tour visitor metaphor*, for instance, should lead designers to elaborate metacommunication by contrasting the user's own culture with the visited culture. However, this was not expressed in alternatives presented by P1.1 and P1.3. Neither their discourse, nor their mockups gave any evidence of contrast. P1.3, for example, said:

```
P1.3: In the guided tour visitor, I would inform the average
of miles per hour that each car covers, as well as the size of
the car. The car details have this information, but I would
include mileage per hour because it is what the guy is used to
seeing. He thinks of speed in miles per hour and the size of
the tank in gallons, because there [in Israel] it is the same
as in Brazil.
```

Although P1.3 was using *the guided tour visitor metaphor* to design an appropriate interface for an American going to Israel, she expressed the cultural variable 'average speed' using *the domestic traveler metaphor*. Part of the problem may have been due to the absence of the word 'contrast' in the definition of the *guided tour visitor metaphor* (which was then included for subsequent experiments).

Likewise, P1.6's question also shows that the main feature of this metaphor (the contrast between two cultures) was unclear:

```
P1.6: In relation to speed limits and ages, for example, in
which metaphors would the Canadian and American values appear
and be contrasted, besides the measurement units themselves?
```

Definitions and examples of other metaphors led to uncertainty, as well. P1.3, for instance, needed examples to help her understand differences between *the observer at a distance* and *the foreigner with translator metaphors*.

```
P1.3: I found it difficult to understand the difference between
the two metaphors [observer at a distance and foreigner with
translator] and it would be very helpful to have examples of
the two to be able to distinguish between this and that case.
```

P1.4 found it difficult to see the difference between *the observer at a distance* and *the guided tour visitor metaphor*:

```
P1.4: I find that these two metaphors [observer at a distance
and guided tour visitor] are very close to each other. [...] But
it is quite difficult to separate one from the other.
```

P1.5's point of view, in turn, was different from the others. It called our attention to a very important new issue. In this participant's view, the continuum of cultural approximation represents "where the user is" (or could be) "positioned" relative to the other culture. Consequently (in his opinion), the farther the distance between the user's position and the foreign culture, the greater the amount of explanations and scaffolds that should be offered to the user.

```
P1.5: If the guy is farther away, then you have to explain
this [in more detail], isn't it? [..] Then, I must make it
clearer, because he is far away.
```

Although P1.5 is correct in diagnosing what a foreign user needs if he or she is culturally very distant from content presented in cross-cultural websites, as explained in Chap. 3 (Sect. 3.1, p. 44) CVM express something different. The five distinct perspectives along a continuum of cultural approximation represent how a designer finds that the user should experience the foreign culture. Very specifically, users may *actually* be quite familiar with some foreign culture and yet, for security reasons already mentioned in previous chapters, designers may decide to use *the domestic traveler metaphor* when, for instance, designing interaction for credit card handling tasks in international e-commerce applications.

Evidence like the illustrated above helped us to improve CVM definitions, contrasts and examples in technical terms. The improvement took more than one round of revision.[5] We began by changing some of the metaphors' names, but then felt the need to improve terms in their definitions and illustrations, so that they would more clearly contrast with each other. All revisions were then consolidated into a single tutorial that was used in subsequent stages of this research.

4.1.1.2   Evidence of the Epistemic Nature of CVM

Epistemic tools and materials are those that can generate new knowledge, not only in factual terms but also in more abstract conceptual terms. Evidence of this category of meanings in the participants' discourse sprang from four specific subcategories related to how CVM led participants into thinking about the problem (not only its potential solutions) and to respond to difficulties they encountered in the re-design activity, namely: (i) mapping of the design space; (ii) exploration of communicative effects achieved by articulating cultural variables with different metaphors; (iii) increased awareness of the designers' own cultural biases and gaps; and, (iv) a kind of mirror effect, when designers placed themselves in the role of recipients of their own design communication.

Regarding (i), the mapping of design space, CVM guided the participants throughout the re-design process, helping them to focus more sharply on culture-related issues and to map out the problem space with higher precision and objectivity.

---

[5] All improvements and revisions in CVM's names and descriptions are available in [12].

P1.1: I was totally guided by the metaphors. [...] When I got mixed up with this metaphor, I looked at this continuous scale and I positioned myself closer to this one, here. [...] The continuum, the separation between metaphors reminded me of the differences.

P1.2: When I was doing the sketching I just tried to keep in mind the explanation for the metaphor and to map the 'real world' scenario in my head to a 'GUI' representation. [...] They make me aware of which information can be shown to users in order to help them adjust their mental models of the workflow.

P1.3: I [was able to] identify better which questions depend on culture, and which ones don't. I dropped the ones that don't depend on culture. Right there I saw it and realized that there were things to be eliminated and things to be added. [...] Then it helped me to understand the problem and to know where I wanted to get to.

P1.4: The moment I became aware of these [cultural] differences, wow! I must [now] think about them.

Regarding (ii), the communicative effects of exploring cultural variables and CVM, the metaphors helped designers in thinking about how to use cultural variables in the context of different metaphors while elaborating metacommunication. P1.1, for instance, realized that cultural variables generate different levels of difficulty in design:

P1.1: Variables like unit of measurement and volume are the most trivial ones to handle [with] your metaphors. It's a piece of cake! Now, the meaning of "economy car" is an important aspect and more difficult than what I did for the foreigner with translator metaphor, and I used it a lot. And [then] the issue of minimum age to drive a car as a rule of business, [same with] the use of the driver's license.

P1.2, in turn, realized that the communication of cultural diversity by promoting intercultural contact may require new forms of representation.

P1.2: These experiences involve other kinds of senses, so the visual representation might not be so effective [as] to hit and impregnate user with the relevant aspects of the cultural values that [the] designer wants to communicate. [...] The 'addendum' information should be presented according to the workflow or interaction with the interface, in a non-obtrusive way. Because information about it is [there] to support, not to [get in the way].

Difficulties in manipulating cultural variables led participants to realize that there are challenges or problems in cross-cultural design that they had not thought of before and that called for solutions. We found evidence that CVM help in raising the designers' awareness about issues that are new to them. P1.1, for instance, had difficulties with the cultural variable 'meaning of economy car'.

P1.1: Regarding the sizes of compact cars and so on […] I
thought of the following: how would the system look like from
the point of view of a British [user]? I would have to reveal
the point of view of Americans. Would it be possible that
Americans think of car size in the same way as the British?
And this question had to be seen from the British point of
view. I actually did not know. I had no idea.

P1.1 also had problems dealing with another cultural variable, language. Since
his targeted user was an American who chooses London for car pick-up, English is
the language spoken on both places. But CVM encouraged P1.1 to think about
language as a cultural variable. He pondered about how users would feel regarding
cultural differences in language use.

P1.1: The fact that both these cultures speak the same language […], because when it comes to the question of the
[translation], how would that [translation] be written in
British English? We look at questions about the variables of
measurement, or currency […], but, at times I did not know
whether I was providing a [translation] or not. If I was to
do that from Portuguese into English, it would be much
easier.

The re-design process with CVM led P1.1, P1.2, P1.3 and P1.4 to consider issues
they had ignored until then.

P1.1: If I hadn't followed the metaphors, I don't know how I
would have been able to think about that. I think I wouldn't have
had the same concerns. And that's for sure. I think that they
bear the promise to make people conscious of cultural issues.

P1.2: I, as a designer, should [keep in mind] that other cultures might interact with my interface. So I should somehow,
maybe at [a] low level, [provide] some information/interac-
tion capabilities to these foreign users. I must identify what
part of the content or interaction flows can be differently
[instantiated] by culture

P1.3: How can we speak of the Israeli culture within the context of the American practice? Certainly, if I hadn't heard
about these metaphors, I would have had difficulty in doing
[the proposed activity] because I wouldn't have been aware of
the problem!

P1.4: This helped me get more informed, that he is closer [to
the other culture]. And this is very important because all the
site has to be able to inform where he is, to inform him of
the context.

As explained in Chap. 3 (Sect. 3.1), CVM are not meant to elicit the cultural
content and variables, but only to design communication about it. However, regarding
(iii), CVM increased awareness of the designers' own cultural biases and gaps,
different participants identified their own lack of knowledge about car rentals as a
possible problem. This is actually a good sign that in real professional activity they
would most probably request to be given this information or go look for it themselves.

P1.1: The fact that I have lived in England makes it easier
for me to understand a little about the car rental system
over there, because I have rented a car there before. But
only a little, because I had only one or two experiences with
car rental there, which was not much. Up to that point, I was
not able to see the cultural differences between the Americans
and the British and when I came here to choose a car, I was
still not able to identify these differences.

P1.6: I was not aware of the age limits to get a driving
license.

Some explained that they did not use a specific cultural variable because they did
not know how to express them in the interface.

P1.4: The meaning of near and far away, I do not know how to
express that.

Cultural gaps experienced by some of the participants actually helped us to
confirm the epistemic potential of CVM in bringing out to the participants
aspects of their own knowledge and perceptions regarding other cultures. At
least two of them (P1.1 and P1.5) decided to seek for knowledge in another
website:

P1.1: I tried to get tips from the [..] AVIS website for the
UK (in theory it follows the rules of that country) and to see
how I could transpose that into the American rules.

P1.5: Thinking about what would be different for the Canadians,
I opened a car rental site from Quebec (which was right there
beside that site) to see how they offered their cars for rent.
I found their site worse than that of AVIS's. But you can
understand a little [more] about the language issue. The first
language they offer is English.

Finally, regarding (iv), a kind of mirror effect, when designers placed themselves
in the role of recipients of their own design communication, CVM led designers
to put themselves more clearly in the role of recipients of the metacommunication
(i.e. as users).

P1.1: How would the system look like from the point of view
of the British? I would have to give the point of view of the
Americans. Would the Americans think of the size of the car in
the same way as the British think? And this question had to
be [asked] in the British way.

P1.2: Actually, I was considering myself as a "gringo" who's
looking for a car rent in Mexico. Yeah, I realize the point
is how the Mexican culture is presented.

P1.3: I imagined the scene that you describe. I imagined that
a friend was going to Israel and had to rent a car. I imagined
that then it would help him to understand the questions [if I
give him] explanations and bring up curiosities from that
country.

Until now we presented evidence that our metaphors helped designers to map out the problem space, to realize that culture is part of a communication process and that as such it deserves attention. From now on, we present evidence of how CVM helped designers to elaborate the metacommunication of a cross-cultural system.

4.1.1.3   Evidence That Metaphors Help Designers to Communicate Cultural Diversity

Evidence shows that participants began by trying to identify which cultural variables should be included and then followed CVM concepts to start the re-design process. P1.3 and P1.5, for instance, inspected all interaction paths to find out which cultural variables were already expressed and which ones could be added.

> P1.3: First of all, I wanted to understand what was necessary for the first screen. Then, I began to ask myself if such things were relevant for Americans and for Israeli. [...] For example, car insurance is not a cultural variable, a child's seat, I do not know. So, some things I could not change because they are already included in the price of the car and so on. But what called my attention is the things that have cultural connotation and that may be different.

> P1.5: At first, I collected the variables that the system is dealing with in each section. The interactive elements, the opportunities for interaction. After that, I had yet another step, another opportunity, wherever there was one missing. And after thinking... there, for each [variable] which of the metaphors applied.

They reviewed CVM concepts in order to decide how to start the re-design itself.

> P1.3: First of all, I went there to see what [the current website] was like. Then I came [to the metaphors table], read these concepts again and decided I would begin with the observer at a distance.

Participants also made decisions about content and expression. P1.2, P1.3 and P1.4, for instance, explained in the post-test interview that they explored specific types of signs and resources (images, videos, maps, color and so on) to express culture or cultural differences.

> P1.2: With the guided tour, I thought that information should be richer, that's why I proposed the [use of] videos with a navigation strip. This [...] was because videos support explanations through time via narrative and you can hit users with more information that can be internalized in a more intuitive way than static information (because there's a story in the video not a mere fact as in the observer at a distance). In simple words, when you are [a] tour guide you point the relevant features about the foreign culture, so [using] videos is in some way the adequate [choice] to talk about the foreign culture.

P1.3: Instead of showing a list where the guy writes where he wants to go, it would be better to have a small map containing such places so that, when he passed the mouse over them, those places would be highlighted and then he would have a notion of the country, of the country's map.

P1.4: I would not use the same color as that of the rest of the site. I would use a different color. I would put a flag of the city or of the country to make it stand out… To send the message that you are in Rio de Janeiro, you see? You can already see things of Rio de Janeiro. If he changes city, he would see everything different.

P1.4: But there would also be the average speed limit of the city, of the roads, also showing the image of a speedometer, because the grading of miles and kilometers is totally different. Here, there is also the option to change into miles.

P1.1, in turn, explained how *the guided tour visitor metaphor* helped him to elaborate metacommunication which avoid breakdowns.

P1.1: Then, so that [the user] is not forced to keep giving information about his credit card to be able to go on, the system acts as a guide explaining to him: '- look, to make a reservation in the United Kingdom you need to have an account with AVIS and show your credit card.

Participants' mockups[6] gave us additional clues about how the metaphors were expressed. Likewise the participants' rhetoric clarified their strategy for defining how to communicate content using each metaphor. The following statements and mockup images illustrate how P1.1 and P1.2, for instance, elaborated the metacommunication message.

P1.1 Examples
P1.1 started the process sketching a re-design alternative guided by *the foreigner with translator metaphor* (see Fig. 4.3). He followed the strategy of expressing cultural variables with this metaphor in the same way as AVIS British website does (http://www.avis.uk), but with 'tips':

P1.1: Then, I chose to put the size and the values that the British site used with caption that the American [user] would like to see. As he is driving a rented car in the UK, then British cars would appear. And when you look for details of the car, I came this far to be able to use all variables. Both the car consumption and the capacity of the tank would appear in liters, that, if I'm not mistaken, it is what is used in Britain.

Figure 4.3 shows how P1.1 associated a tip in parentheses ("small (compact)", "mini (sub-compact)", etc.) to each car size classification in this alternative.

---

[6] The whole set of participants' mockups is available in [1212].

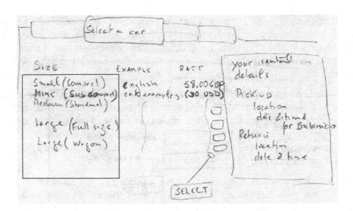

Fig. 4.3 P1.1's mockup guided by the foreigner with translator metaphor: 'Select a car' webpage

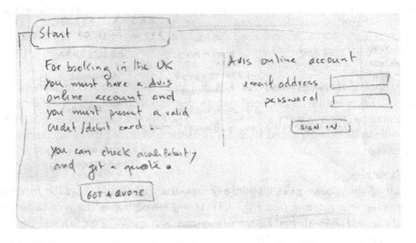

Fig. 4.4 P1.1's mockup guided by the guided tour visitor metaphor: 'Home page'

With *the guided tour visitor metaphor*, P1.1 used the strategy of guiding the user with tips (see Fig. 4.4).

P1.1: As in the 'foreigner with translator', the designer does it the way it is done abroad, which forces the guy to follow the procedure used abroad. Here [with the guided tour visitor] I keep wondering that there is someone helping him, a cultural guide. Then, so that [the user] is not forced to keep giving information about his credit card to be able to go on, the system acts as a guide explaining to him: '- look, to make a reservation in the United Kingdom you need to have an account with AVIS and show your credit card'. I am assuming that there is a difference in the way the rental is done in the USA and in Britain and I am explaining that right from the start.

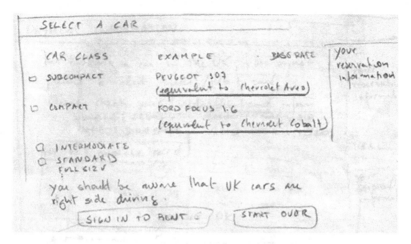

Fig. 4.5 P1.1's mockup guided by the guided tour visitor metaphor: 'Select a car' webpage

P1.1 also followed the strategy of contrasting the visited culture with users' culture (see Fig. 4.5).

P1.1: And then, after he chooses the car and fills in dates and place, the information about the car is shown and, in truth, the novelty shown here is the [car] classes that I kept the same as those in American standards. But in the examples of cars [belonging in each class], they are British cars, those you will find there, in London. But it gives the equivalent of an American car for [the American user] to have an idea. It would be exactly that car, this car is equivalent to a Chevrolet…

P1.1 discourse about this alternative demonstrates that his choice of using cultural variables from the American or British culture was a conscious one. Figure 4.5 shows how P1.1 contrasted the British car models to American models.

P1.2 Examples

Regarding the alternative proposed by P1.2 guided by *the observer at a distance metaphor* (see Fig. 4.6), he said:

P1.2: working with the observer at a distance metaphor was the easiest and most comfortable way to solve it because you can practically bring to users whatever you want, [packaged as] information chunks.

Figure 4.7 shows in details how P1.2 grouped relevant information in the 'Do you know…' section of his proposed 'Home page' mockup guided by *the observer at distance metaphor* (Fig. 4.6). This section includes cultural variables such as the minimum legal age to drive, speed limits and driving rules and conventions. P1.2 tried to "represent it in a pleasant and [least] obtrusive way possible".

With *the guided tour visitor metaphor*, P1.2 explored different types of signs to explain the foreign culture to the user.

Fig. 4.6 P1.2's mockup guided by the observer at a distance metaphor: 'Home page'

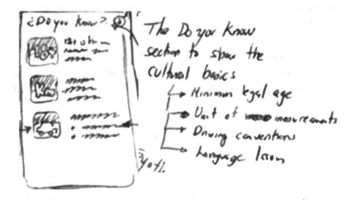

Fig. 4.7 Portion of P1.2's mockup guided by the observer at a distance metaphor

P1.2: the second case is to detect the core cultural aspects
that are [related to] a particular variable. Therefore you can
construct the "story" for explaining. The "fingering" is [the]
equivalent [of marking] what is important through the narrative. In the video examples, that would involve zooms, particular fragments of narration, clarity on movements, cultural
gestures, landscape features, etc.

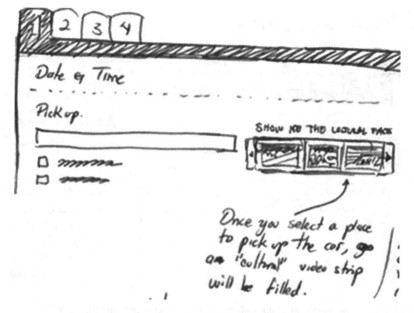

Fig. 4.8 P1.2's mockup guided by the guided tour visitor metaphor: 'Home page'

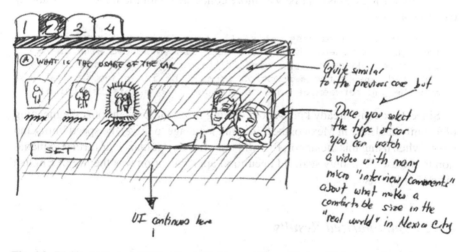

Fig. 4.9 P1.2's mockup guided by the guided tour visitor metaphor: 'Select a car' page

In his first screen P1.2 offered opportunities for intercultural contact through cultural videos associated with driving rules and conventions (see Fig. 4.8). In the second screen he explored the meaning of a comfortable car in Mexico (see Fig. 4.9).

Using concepts associated with *the foreigner with translator metaphor*, P1.2 realized that the user will be in touch with an unfamiliar environment since the interface

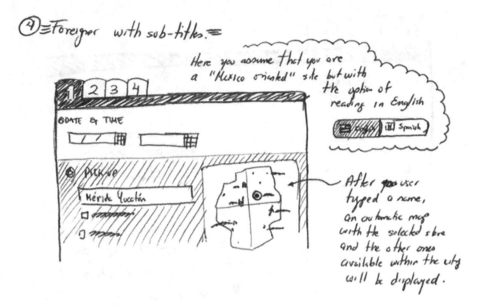

Fig. 4.10 P1.2's homepage mockup guided by the foreigner with translator metaphor

is actually for Mexicans. But he was more concerned with the interface's usability (see Fig. 4.10[7]).

> P1.2: In the third case, it's all about looking better for the foreign user. Then, the current user is confronted with an odd interface. However, [a] certain level of understanding [is expected] under the assumption [that] the interface is usable and the gap between designer's and user's semiosis is minimal.

Since Mexicans already know about driving rules and conventions, the meaning of a comfortable car in Mexico, the minimum legal age to drive, the speed limits and so on, when using this metaphor, P1.2 did not offer any guidance or further explanation to the user. The only scaffold in cultural approximation was the use of English instead of Spanish.

4.1.2 Summarized Results

Step One was carried out for two reasons. The first one was to assess the potential of CVM when designers use them to create re-design alternatives. The other was to assess the HCI designers' and evaluators' understanding and use of CVM. Evidence collected in Step One pointed out that: (i) CVM should be improved to minimize difficulties in understanding the fundamental concepts associated with them;

---

[7] In this figure, the old name of the metaphor ("foreigner with sub-titles") appears on top. Information about changes on CVM's names and descriptions (motivated by empirical evaluation) are available in [12].

(ii) CVM achieve considerable epistemic effect in a cross-cultural design process; and, (iii) CVM help designers in organizing communication about intentionally displayed opportunities for intercultural contact.

Difficulties in understanding CVM led us to improve them. Metaphor definitions presented in Chap. 3 (see Sect. 3.1 p. 44) already include the following: elaboration of a single domain tutorial to illustrate all metaphors (a hypothetical website with cooking recipes); creation of a practical how-to guide for those interested in applying the metaphors; revision of design metacommunication features for each metaphor to emphasize the differences between all metaphors; revision of metaphor names. The revised CVM were used in Step Two.

The epistemic nature of CVM while guiding designers throughout the re-design process was also verified. They helped the designers to focus on cultural aspects (apart from numerous other interaction design aspects) and to map out the design problem more precisely.

CVM also supported participating designers in thinking about how to communicate culture-related content, which cultural variables to express and how. The adoption of each metaphor brings about different effects (cultural isolation, cultural mediation or cultural immersion) and led to specific forms of organization of the interactive discourse. Designers clearly realized that the design space was substantially expanded once they had to choose between five different metaphors to guide their interpretations and decisions.

Further evidence collected in this experiment (see below) revealed that challenges in manipulating cultural variables lead designers to: think about distinctions that they were not aware of or would not necessarily bring to bear in cross-cultural design; and find out how to solve these challenges. The epistemic value of CVM in teasing out the designers' cultural gaps and increasing their awareness about some implications of cultural diversity in cross-cultural design was thus evidenced.

Finally, by exploring alternative cultural perspectives and communicating them through re-designed interaction, designers made conscious decisions regarding content and expression in communication. Participants' discourse and mockups reveal that they went far beyond transposing examples provided in the tutorial (for another domain). They clearly explored other types of signs to communicate foreign culture material to their hypothetical user stereotype. Even when designers faced difficulties due to cultural gaps, evidence collected in this experiment strongly suggests that CVM helped them bridge the gaps and re-elaborate an interactive discourse to communicate cultural diversity.

4.2   Step Two: Cultural Viewpoint Metaphors at Evaluation Time

The purpose of this step was to evaluate the potential of CVM as an inspection tool for early formative HCI evaluation at re-design time. The following research question guided our investigation: "Can CVM help HCI evaluators in focusing inspection on cultural issues (apart from others)? How?"

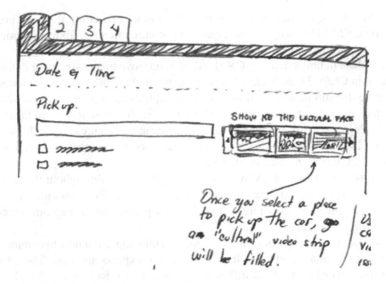

Fig. 4.11 P1.2's handmade mockup

In Step One, designers proposed three re-design alternatives by sketching handmade mockups for each one of the following metaphors: *the observer at a distance*, *the guided tour visitor* and *the foreigner with translator*. We selected two sets of alternatives[8] (one by P1.2 and the other by P1.4) to see how HCI evaluators interpret designs produced using CVM. The selection criterion was the richness of the drawings in giving evidence of metaphors and opportunities for intercultural contact.

We reproduced the handmade mockups by P1.2 and P1.4 with Balsamiq.[9] Balsamiq mockups had the advantage of standardizing the visual quality of designs and factoring out judgment that might be influenced by the designers' ability to draw nice sketches. Figures 4.11 and 4.12 show an example of a handmade sketch and its corresponding Balsamiq mockup.

We created three interactive Balsamiq mockups for each one of the participants' sets: one for *the observer at a distance* design, one for *the guided tour visitor* design and one for *the foreigner with translator* design.

There were four participants (P2.1, P2.2, P2.3 and P2.4) in Step Two, all nationals of the same country (Brazil). All had good experience in HCI and reading fluency in English. P2.1, P2.2 and P2.3 had further professional experience in HCI projects than P2.4 (see Table 4.2).

The experiment took place at the Department of Informatics at PUC-Rio, with a duration of two and a half hours. A preliminary questionnaire with questions

---

[8] Although we selected two sets of mockups, pilot tests showed that using just one set of alternatives per participant would be enough to answer our research question. Furthermore, they showed that the experiment was too long with two alternatives, since each set required different scenarios of inspection and hence different evaluation questionnaires.

[9] Balsamiq© (http://www.balsamiq.com) is sketching tool by Balsamiq Studios, LLC.

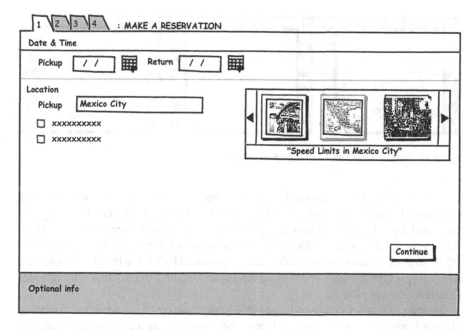

Fig. 4.12 P1.2' Balsamiq mockup

Table 4.2 The distribution of alternatives and scenario among participants

Id	Nationality	Alternatives proposed by…	Inspection scenario: an American residing in the USA chooses a place in…
P2.1	Brazilian	P1.2 (Mexican designer)	Mexico for the car pick-up.
P2.2	Brazilian	P1.2 (Mexican designer)	Mexico for the car pick-up.
P2.3	Brazilian	P1.4 (Brazilian designer)	Brazil for the car pick-up.
P2.4	Brazilian	P1.4 (Brazilian designer)	Brazil for the car pick-up.

about their experience abroad and their professional (or other) practice with HCI evaluation was collected by email prior to the experiment. After the researcher presented the experiment goals, the following sequential activities were carried out:

1. The researcher introduced CVM.
2. The participant used CVM to inspect one set of Balsamiq mockups from Step One in accordance with a compatible scenario (see Table 4.2).
3. The researcher carried out a post-test interview.

In the general scenario we used for this experiment, the participant plays the role of a professional working in a project to re-design the Avis website. His or her goal is to evaluate a set of alternatives (produced by P1.2 or P1.4 in the previous step), taking into consideration that the designers tried to use one predominant metaphor in each one of the alternatives. They should also keep in mind that designers had the explicit design intent of promoting different levels of user awareness about cultural diversity in the rent-a-car domain.

Fig. 4.13 Videos of click-through Balsamiq mockups

The set of re-design alternatives were randomly distributed to participants as presented in Table 4.2. Because P2.1 and P2.2 evaluated the set of alternatives proposed by P1.2 (a Mexican designer), their inspection scenario involved an American residing in the USA who chooses Mexico for the car pick-up. P2.3 and P2.4, in turn, evaluated the set of alternatives proposed by P1.4 (a Brazilian designer). Their inspection scenario involved an American residing in the USA who chooses Brazil for the car pick-up.

In order to avoid distractions by possible interaction problems while manipulating Balsamiq mockups, we produced videos where the presumed user interacts with the click-through Balsamiq mockups (see Fig. 4.13). Each evaluator could thus focus on what was really important: the evaluation of interaction that he or she observed in the videos.

Participants were then invited to answer three evaluation questionnaires (A, B and C), one for each interaction video. This was the physical record of evaluation results. The questionnaires included questions about which cultural variables were used as well as from which culture (the user's or foreign) they were borrowed. Additional questions focused on the kind of interface signs and interaction forms that were used to communicate cultural differences such as text, video, images, comparisons, and so on.

The questionnaires' goal was actually twofold. First, we intended to guide the evaluators throughout the inspection by asking questions about the fundamentals of CVM, cultural variables and metacommunication features. The evaluator should be able to report evidence of a specific metaphor by answering which cultural variables were expressed through the "interface", and which interface elements were used to communicate cultural differences.

Second, we wanted to capture the evaluators' preliminary interpretation about the quality of metacommunication considering that the presumed design intent was promoting the users' contact with cultural diversity.

Once they completed their evaluation, participants reported verbally on the evaluation process as the researcher conducted a post-test interview. This stage aimed at colleting mainly the participants' discourse about: (i) their evaluation results; (ii) the evaluation process, i.e., how the proposed metaphors helped them (if at all) in focusing and thinking on the quality of metacommunication; (iii) what they found easy or difficult to do; and, (iv) what they learned (if anything) with the experiment.

4.2.1   Detailed Results

In this section we present the main results from Step Two. The main categories of analysis from our interpretation during the analysis process are: (i) difficulties faced during the evaluation process; (ii) evidence of the epistemic nature of CVM at evaluation time; and, (iii) evidence that metaphors help designers to inspect and evaluate the communicability of cultural diversity.

4.2.1.1   Difficulties Faced During the Evaluation Process

Although evidence does not suggest relevant difficulties in understanding the gist of CVM, this category of analysis led us into further issues that should be better explained to facilitate the evaluation process. They have to do with: the design intent; the object of evaluation (expression or content); and the differences between interface element, cultural practice and cultural variable. Furthermore, participants had difficulties to conclude the evaluation process.

Regarding design intent, some participants said that they did not know how to say what was right or wrong because the scenario we gave them did not tell them specifically about design intent details.

> P2.2: With the foreigner with translator, I felt much more 'inside' Mexico. This made sense here. But would it be that my contractor wished to create this sensation? Or would it be that he wanted an observer at a distance, instead?

> P2.3: My regret is because I do not know what to consider right or wrong. I don't know if it should be the 'domestic traveler', if this is good or bad, I don't know which one was [actually intended].

For, P2.1, in turn, the object of evaluation was not clear, she did not know whether she had to inspect and evaluate interface signs as expressions or as what they stand for (content).

> P2.1: For me '18+' is not something from my culture, so I can imagine that it should be from some of those [other] cultures. For example, in the USA, [if you are] older than 16 years you can drive. Then, if it is showing 'above 18', it is because this is in Mexico. [...] So you wanted me to see not exactly the sign on the interface, but what it should stand for?

Regarding the differences between interface element and cultural variable, we realized that they should be clarified and exemplified. In the proposed scenario for Step Two we presented only the cultural variables that were used by designers in Step One. Such was the case with language, the minimum legal age to drive, speed limits and drivers' license use and conditions. However, we should have also explained that the interface 'elements' for inspection are the interface signs. Anything on the interface that represents something to someone, be it an image, some interface color, a portion of text, a word, just anything. P2.2 and P2.4, for instance, had difficulties in grasping the differences between those concepts.

> P2.2: Cultural practice, cultural variable, design element that represents, that emphasizes cultural differences. These names are very similar, so I got lost. Here, she is talking about the interface, about the concept, about the culture. I had to think to be able to answer: 'What is a variable and what is an interface element?' It is difficult to see what it means to use a variable here, what it is to use an interface element.

> P2.4: I was somewhat confused about what a cultural variable was. Was it a theme, a general topic or a point in....[the interface]. Sometimes, I was almost pointing at the site, you see? I know that it is not about that. But I managed to get organized. For example, the cultural variable I called it 'laws' and then, that way, I could locate which were the 'laws' of the local culture, which were presented there, you see? Then, like 'behavior': there is an example. I think 'behavior' is a cultural variable and there it was, one of the things I had doubts about.

Besides that, some evaluators had difficulties to conclude the evaluation, since they felt a lack of scaffolds to help them in concluding whether the design intent had been reached or not.

> P2.3: I think that there was something missing to support me in my judgment of value. I managed to see if there is a sign or not. You know those things about communication breakdowns, about mistakes. You told me something like: 'Interpret it in this way!' Now, what is the problem in this interpretation? I couldn't do it. I didn't even think about this type of thing. I didn't make any value judgment about that. I could only verify if it communicates or doesn't communicate [the idea]. I didn't make any [further] judgment […]. Then, I think that part of the judgment is missing. I don't know if it is something like a communication breakdown, I don't know. Something in that direction, to support my judgment [process].

> P2.3: Because I find that, in terms of evaluation method, I think I can do the data collection and a good part of the interpretation. And then, what is missing in the interpretation is the judgment of values, and how I go on about my outlook on that re-design.

> P2.3: I think that there is something missing in terms of communication breakdowns. Where does this communication fail here? Then, if I had this goal, which one is this metaphor? If my goal was to communicate the comparison, why didn't I make the comparison correctly?

> P2.4: But there was a failure. For example, you said that it is observer at a distance, but [there was no place to say] what is your evaluation regarding the use of the metaphor for

his design? Something more direct, like this. In the end, we
make it here, but there is no explicit question, there is
nothing saying you really used it… In the end it is here. So
much so, that I found that… I was expecting this question! I
tried to fit this in here [in the evaluation questionnaire].
To explain that.

Despite all difficulties, CVM helped participants to say which alternative is more
appropriate given the scenario they had to use.

P2.1: I would put [alternative] 'B' with some things from 'A'.
But, this way, if I had to choose one of the three, I would
choose 'B' as it is. But if I could change something, I would
add some things of 'A' to 'B'. […] I thought that the second one made the comparisons. It located the user in his
culture, but at the same time it was there making comparisons
and showing other things, even in a more interesting form.

P2.4: Certainly, it was 'B'. I even justified it there. When
you work with comparison, when you show it, it is an even
richer form of knowing.

And participants could think over the general benefits of CVM in evaluating
and designing cross-cultural applications. See how P2.2 and P2.3 manifest their
impression. P2.2, in particular, recognizes the importance of naming elements of
the problem.

P2.2: Perhaps, to sum up, to give a final opinion, to close the
analysis, to name everything that I was talking about [the
metaphors are good].

P2.3: I think [the metaphors] stimulate, they may stimulate,
they have the potential to stimulate [your thinking] at various levels, at different levels, because they are different.

Most categories of meaning presented here are not related to difficulties in understanding the idea of CVM (as the category Difficulties of Step One). Instead, they
indicate some issues to be improved to facilitate the evaluation process. The main
issue is the lack of scaffolds to help evaluators in concluding the evaluation process.
Evidence showed, for instance, that the evaluation questionnaire could be improved
by including a specific question or section about the quality of designer-to-user
metacommunication.

4.2.1.2   Evidence of the Epistemic Nature of CVM at Evaluation Time

The epistemic nature of CVM could also be traced at evaluation. The analysis of
empirical evidence showed that CVM helped evaluators in: (i) interpreting their
findings throughout the inspection; (ii) realizing that cross-cultural content and HCI
design may be addressed separately at design time; and, (iii) examining communicative strategies and new possibilities in cross-cultural HCI re-design.

Participants like P2.2, P2.3 and P2.4 explained how CVM guided their interpretation during inspection, since CVM organized the problem space.

P2.3: Oh, yes! Because [the metaphors] guided me to the kind of interpretation that I would do for the signs […]. They helped me because they called my attention to this other class of signs and also guided me to the sort of interpretation I would get.

P2.3: The metaphors called my attention to which ones are cultural signs. I interpreted these signs according to the metaphors: [checking] if they inform, compare or only transcribe [information] into another language, into another culture. It helped me a lot in this sense.

P2.4: I started to think by myself and got mixed up. If you organize your thoughts […] from what you see to what the user gained with that in terms of contact, then these [the metaphors and the evaluation questionnaire] certainly do help. If your intention is to promote intercultural contact, then, the metaphors and the questionnaire help.

P2.2: If you had not given me anything, nothing like that, and got me sitting here in front of the computer saying "Please evaluate this!", the result would not be as rich as the one that came out because you gave me a tool […] to reflect [with]. You did not just throw me in here and said: Do the evaluation! This helped me to reflect about cultural issues.

Participants' cultural gaps regarding the scenario where an American residing in the USA chooses a pick-up location in Mexico (for P2.1 and P2.2) or Brazil (for P2.3 and P2.4) also led them into improving their knowledge about intercultural content and HCI design segmentation at design time. They realized that cross-cultural HCI designers should have some level of 'awareness' about cultural diversity, although it is not required that they know of all the existing differences.

P2.1: So, I think I should know at least a little bit about each one of the cultures to be able to answer question 3.[10]

P2.2: This will make a difference in evaluation. I do not belong to culture A or B, I am from culture C. This [must] also check the impact it will have on the evaluation too, doesn't it? Because the domain was simple. But there may be a more complicated domain or another domain where he does not see that there is [cultural] metacommunication there because he doesn't know culture A or B. But how will he see that that is metacommunication [about culture]? This has to be taken into consideration.

P2.3: Then the knowledge that someone has about the domain and a little about the cultures may turn this type of evaluation into [something] more or less difficult. So, about this case

---

[10] Question 3 in the evaluation questionnaire asks the participant to check whether listed variables were presented for culture A or B.

in particular, I couldn't even identify if it is one or the
other because I don't know much about the Brazilian culture.
There, it is more about the domain and not about the culture.
I don't know the American domain and culture. I think these
two things may influence the analysis and so, knowing the difference between my own knowledge problems and interface problems, requires that the evaluator be more attentive to this
type of thing.

It has been also realized, however, that cultural gaps are part of the design problem
in intercultural domains, not a deficiency of CVM.

P2.3: I think the difficulties, the negative points ... I think
that it is inherent to the problem itself, which is to evaluate something that involves different cultures and that the
evaluator doesn't know about. I don't know whether it is a
more difficult problem than that of [having enough] domain
knowledge. Because with the domain things are more explicit,
but with culture things are more implicit, which is more tacit
knowledge. People do [things] and act simply because they are
used to doing so, from when they were young children. But they
are never aware of that fact. I think that tacit knowledge of
culture is even worse than domain [knowledge]. I think that
the greatest difficulty is this, but I think it is part of the
problem and not [a drawback] of the method.

CVM-based formative evaluation focused on intercultural issues also led some
evaluators to start thinking as designers. P2.3, for instance, wonders about ways to
communicate cultural diversity through metacommunication:

P2.3: [...] like having to click on a link to open another window [with cultural information]. To have one window where only
the information is shown and another window to see the differences and the comparison. And getting out of this one to
go to this other one [requires] some extra work [...] Then the
user will go there only if he wants to.

For P2.1, the very concept of five cultural viewpoint metaphors opens up different
possibilities in cross-cultural HCI design and evaluation:

P2.1: I found it very interesting to divide [the problem with]
these metaphors, to have this view rather than to be either
in his culture or in ours, to have these intermediary levels.
This is much better than [thinking of] it only [as] in either
his culture or in mine.

Finally, participants thought about how metaphors can help them to address solutions
for the HCI re-design. P2.1, for instance, declares that CVM can help to identify the
specific portion to be re-designed:

P2.1: The fact that they are well defined helps me to detect
this difference even more when I am comparing one [alterna-
tive] that is of one type with the other that is of another
type. For example, in one re-design [proposal] I could see
that if I had... [if] my first system was system A and I wanted

it to be [system] C,[11] I would just know what I must elaborate
[this point]. I know [what I want] is a characteristic of
that and I can replace it for this one. So, I think that it
can help me in this way.

In conclusion, with this category of analysis we collected evidence that CVM
helped participants to begin to attend to previously undetected cultural issues and
their implications for the HCI design process.

4.2.1.3   Evidence That Metaphors Help Designers to Inspect and Evaluate the Communicability of Cultural Diversity

HCI evaluation methods usually focus on specific qualities: usability [5, 9, 10],
communicability [3, 4, 11], culturability [1], accessibility [7, 14] and so on.
Likewise, our challenge was to see whether CVM could help evaluators to focus on
the communicability of cultural issues.

According to participants, the evaluation process was achieved in three major steps.
First, participants identified which cultural variables were used by the designers:

P2.3: First of all, I checked if it was a cultural variable,
if it mentioned anything about the culture, and then I made
the analysis of what the designer was saying about that variable. I did this one by one.

Second, they tried to classify to which culture those variables belonged.

P2.1: For me '18+' is not something from my culture, so I can
imagine that it should be from some of those [other] cultures.
For example, in the USA, [if you are] older than 16 years you
can drive. Then, if it is showing 'above 18', it is because
this is in Mexico.

P2.3: In the last one, in C [foreigner with translator],
although it is written in English, he used 'R$' and not 'BRL'.
I would rather have it as it is in English, I would rather use
'BRL'. And then he used 'R$', because he is thinking about the
local currency, only the content of that culture translated.
But I would also translate currency into its denomination in
the other language. But it remains 'Real'. I would change only
that, but I am not sure if I would change the perspective.

Third, participants inspected and evaluated how cultural variables were communicated: by comparing, contrasting, informing and so on. The comparison between
the three alternatives was important at this stage.

P2.1: This is the video from guided tour visitor, so, here, I
expected to see [the metaphor leading to comparison], to see
the two things. Although it appears in the user's language,

---

[11] The participant refers to the A, B and C mockups presented as part of the materials for this
experiment (Figure 4.13).

he is showing me a measurement unit that is not [the user's
preference]. And also, there is no information here. I found
that the first video was more guided tour visitor than observer
at a distance, and this video more observer at a distance than
guided tour visitor. This is because [in the first video] I saw
more comparisons.

P2.2: [To check] if the variable is in the perspective of the
user or of the other culture makes a difference when evaluating the project. [It helps] not because it is metaphor 1, 2,
3 or 5. What makes the difference [is to check] if it is in this
or in that perspective, if it is contrasting [things] or not.

P2.3: I analyzed the interface, saw that he talked explicitly
about information, about another culture, 'local info' [for
example]. And there, there is information in this other culture that I did not have in mine. That is "mine" considering
myself as an American, you see? There was no information for
the American user and, I noticed that this was information
from a different culture. I began to check if he [the designer]
only informed, if he compared, if he informed things from the
user's culture or that other culture.

P2.1 and P2.4, for instance, said that the possibility of comparing five cultural
perspectives also helped them:

P2.1: I found it very interesting to have those points between
1 and 5, so that we can focus our work and evaluate, have that
comparison. Because, otherwise, it would be only 0 or 1. [...].
I found it very cool to have this in mind, to make the comparison. I liked it, I found it very interesting.

P2.4: And when you are evaluating, knowing that these [cul-
tural] variables exist, you are - I'm not saying 'directing'
your thought to one or another [metaphor] - but you 'know'
that there is a variation.

Additionally, the comparison between alternatives led P2.1 to identify relevant
issues:

P2.1: As each metaphor has its own specific characteristic,
they are very different from each other. For example, in this
last one [foreigner with translator], one of the things I saw
in the 1st [video], the 2nd [video] and when I saw the 3rd
video... I was looking for this thing about measurement unit,
which appears on the other videos. I didn't see it. I would
know that if it is 'foreigner with translator', if I saw it
in the Mexican culture there, then it belonged there, in the
[Mexican] culture. Then, in this way, since I didn't see this,
then this could mean that there is something relevant missing
in this interface.

This last evidence confirmed the benefits of comparing alternatives, because it
may lead evaluators into give meaning to the *absence* of something in one design
alternative, compared to its *presence* in another alternative.

Results regarding evidence that metaphors help designers to inspect and evaluate the communicability of cultural diversity are based on specific sub-categories of meanings evidenced in the participants' discourse: (i) focus on the communicability of cultural issues throughout the evaluation process; (ii) mapping of interface elements; and (iii) naming and framing of participants' findings in light of CVM.

Regarding the first sub-category, P2.2 and P2.3 implied that CVM helped them focusing on the communicability of cultural diversity.

> P2.2: I didn't even look to see if it was the best solution in terms of interface [design] itself. I looked only at the cultural issues.

> P2.3: I think it did zoom in. As I said before, I found it hard to go back and analyze the issues [having to do with] interaction and task. I was so engrossed, so stuck within the culture [perspective], that the interaction part [was left out]. [...] It is different when you analyze interaction problems [compared to analyzing problems related to] culture. And I managed to focus on the culture [aspects] of this experiment now.

CVM also helped in (ii), mapping of interface elements. P2.1, for instance, said that he could tag the interface with Communicability Evaluation Method [3, 4, 11] utterances.

> P2.1: I found this interesting to help me understand this part here.[..] As if it were really about those [communicability evaluation] tags. I am going to look at the interface and I am going to put those tags there. And at the end I will see if it is more like one or more like the other. If I want it to be 2 [observer at a distance], then I will get whatever there is of 3 [guided tour visitor], here, and change. I found it very cool because, then, I can make a map of my interface in this way. I found it very interesting and super positive.

P2.3, in turn, said that with the inspection activity proposed by using CVM, he realized that cultural interface elements could be grouped into a specific class of signs.

> P2.3: Since you asked me to make an inspection thinking of communicability, I was inspired by [the methods of Semiotic Engineering], and to analyze the signs. But, for me, this here is another class of signs. Because you are interested in another aspect of communicability.

P2.3 went further into thinking about how to detect communicative breakdowns, which is the purpose of the Communicability Evaluation Methods referred above:

> P2.3: To answer this question [in the evaluation question-naire] I think that there is something missing in terms of communication breakdowns. Where does this communication fail here? Then, if I had this goal, which one is this metaphor? If my goal was to communicate the comparison, why didn't I make the comparison correctly? [...] If [the designer] wanted to follow this metaphor, has he followed it or not? If it was about that other one, has he followed it or not?

It is noteworthy that another participant (P2.4) came up with a specific communicative breakdown in *the foreigner with translator* alternative, which actually opens up opportunities for future work, bringing together CVM and other Semiotic Engineering methods [4, 11] to evaluate what is the impact of CVM-based design on cross-cultural systems users.

> P2.4: By the time I got to option C, when I saw the AVIS Brasil
> flag and Brasil written with an S, then I immediately thought:
> 'this is going to be total immersion'. But the language was
> English! Then I thought: 'Ah! Then it must be the foreigner with
> translator, definitely'. But then I think I found a metacommu-
> nication mistake, not a mistake with using the metaphor. You
> sort of expect if. Both, I as an evaluator and in this case as
> also the user, you sort of expect that you are in this metaphor,
> but you are not. Beginning with the language: it would have to
> be in the other culture's [idiom], but it is in English.

Finally, regarding the third sub-category, evaluators interpreted their findings in light of CVM. Although P2.3 said that they identified the differences between alternatives by just interpreting the interface signs with metaphors concepts, evidence suggests that concepts and examples of metaphors and questions from the evaluation questionnaire guided the evaluation just as much.

> P2.4: The questions [in the questionnaire] help you think. And
> there, there is no way out: you end up coming here [to the
> metaphors table]. We can see it […] that in the end we end up
> learning the idea of the metaphors. Just by looking at them
> and analyzing them you already identify which metaphor the
> designer wanted to follow.

With CVM, participants could name the object of inspection more precisely.

> P2.4: By the time I got to option C, when I saw the AVIS Brasil
> flag and Brasil written with an S, then I immediately thought:
> 'this is going to be total immersion'. But the language was
> English! Then I thought: 'Ah! Then it must be the foreigner
> with translator, definitely'.

> P2.1: I found that the first video was more guided tour visitor
> than observer at a distance, and this video more observer at
> a distance than guided tour visitor. This is because there
> [in the first video] I saw more comparisons.

In conclusion, discourse analysis revealed that all participants agreed that CVM helped them to focus on intercultural issues and that the evaluation activity by interpreting their findings in light of CVM was pleasant and interesting.

4.2.2   Summarized Results

This empirical study was carried out to assess the potential of CVM at evaluation time. Difficulties faced during the evaluation process gave us practical results to improve the CVM documents and scaffolds. Evidence made us realize that the presumed designers' intent should be more detailed when CVM is used in evaluation contexts. Likewise, in order to avoid difficulties, inspection scenarios should provide further information such as a clear description of the design goal. Some evaluators also found it difficult to conclude the evaluation process, they complained about the lack of scaffolds to help them achieve this last step.

Nevertheless, evidence suggests that CVM has leveraged epistemic activity at evaluation time and led HCI practitioners into evaluating five distinct communication strategies that they can use to promote intercultural contact.

The epistemic nature of CVM was manifested once again as participants told us about their thoughts and reflections, about what they learned, how they dealt with challenges and so on. Evidence showed that CVM helped evaluators in interpreting their inspection findings. They realized that intercultural content and HCI design may be segmented into separate layers at design time and thought about communicative strategies and new possibilities to be used in cross-cultural HCI re-design.

Regarding the potential of CVM to help evaluators while inspecting and evaluating the communicability of metacommunication about cultural diversity, Step Two showed that CVM concepts and examples, as well as the evaluation questionnaire, helped evaluators to inspect alternatives in a systematic way. Participants were guided by CVM and they were able to focus narrowly on the communicability of cultural issues by: identifying interface elements and their corresponding cultural variables; answering from which culture (the user's or foreign) the cultural variables were borrowed; and inspecting which cultural perspective(s) was (were) used to communicate cultural variables. Evaluators always interpreted their findings in the light of CVM. Concepts and examples of metaphors and questions in the evaluation questionnaire guided the evaluation process.

4.3   Final Analysis and Synthesis of Results

The reported case study with the Avis website was carried out to assess the comprehension of CVM by HCI designers and evaluators, as well as the potential of CVM in designing and evaluating cross-cultural applications. We aimed at investigating how HCI practitioners appropriate CVM concepts when thinking about cross-cultural design and how CVM helped them to organize the problem space (if at all).

Results from two experiments made in this case study complemented each other. In both of them we found evidence of the epistemic effect of CVM on cross-cultural design and evaluation processes. CVM guided participants throughout the re-design process by helping them focus narrowly on culture, map out the problem space and interpret their findings.

Furthermore, this case study showed another epistemic feature of CVM, its potential to lead participants into segmenting things that are hard to dissociate when looking at interaction with cross-cultural HCI applications: cultural content and metacommunication about cultural content. At design time, CVM helped participants to separate these and concentrate on communication design rather than content selection.

Participants have learned to do this in the process, as they: (1) realized that culture is part of the metacommunication process that happens in HCI; (2) examined five different possibilities for communicating culture; and (3) analyzed the effects entailed by the adoption of each metaphor for organizing interactive discourse.

In conclusion, the five metaphors were not used to generate direct answers to the design problem, but to boost the problem solvers' understanding of the issues involved and the problem itself. Evidence shows that, with CVM, they explored underlying implications, generated alternative solutions and evaluated them against each other. Additionally CVM helped them to name and frame the design problem, a valued step in reflective design activity [13].

In addition to finding a way to organize our own research space in the area of cross-cultural HCI, we also captured evidence and practical advice from the experiment, especially in the context of HCI evaluation. Specifically, we gathered relevant information about how to make CVM become more operational in supporting cross-cultural design and evaluation.

4.4 Triangulation

Results obtained with the case study on Avis website could only be considered new valid knowledge for HCI researchers and professionals after triangulation, the typical validation procedure used in qualitative research [2, 4, 6]. For this purpose, we carried out a new experiment, using CVM in evaluation activity. The triangulation was made by changing the system domain and purpose. While the case study was done in the car rental domain, this new experiment was done in the football domain. We used the Fédération Internationale de Football Association website©.[12] This website, just as AVIS, was not elaborated with CVM and it is clearly a cross-cultural system that can be re-designed to promote intercultural contact. That is, in re-designing (portions of) FIFA website, we can try to use CVM to organize the users' intercultural experience, at various levels of cultural approximation.

We recruited only two participants for this triangulation experiment, given that its purpose was only to cross-check the findings of previous more extensive experiments. As recruiting criteria, we required only that they have good experience in HCI evaluation and reading fluency in English. The two participants, separately, listened to a tutorial introducing the CVM and then inspected the FIFA website following the proposed scenario for this experiment. They were asked to use CVM to guide their evaluation. Once they finished the process, we made a brief individual post-test interview with them.

As was the case with previous experiments, the empirical evidence from this one was the participants' discourse about the evaluation process and product, as well as the participants' impressions and opinions expressed during the post-test interview.

---

[12] www.fifa.com. From now on we will refer to it in abbreviated form as "the FIFA website".

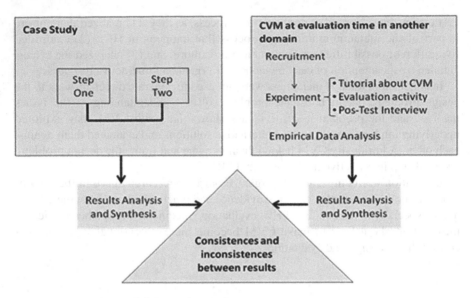

Fig. 4.14 Triangulation: CVM at evaluation time

This data was analyzed with the same discourse analysis techniques [8] used in the AVIS case study. However, whereas in Step One and Step Two we used this method to discover previously unknown discourse categories, now we used it to verify that previously discovered categories recurred in new discourse material. Thus, the validation of our research findings was obtained by triangulating the categories presented in Sects. 1.1 and 1.2 with the results of this final experiment (see Fig. 4.14).

4.4.1   Evaluating FIFA Website with CVM

The International Federation of Association Football, commonly known by the acronym FIFA, "is the international governing body of association football, futsal and beach football. With 208 associations affiliated to FIFA today, world football's governing body has rightly been dubbed the 'United Nations of Football".[13] FIFA has the responsibility of reaching out and touching all corners of the world, using football as a symbol of hope and integration with the following mission: "Develop the game, touch the world, build a better future".

FIFA website presents news, national associations, announces competitions, results, fixtures, development and so on. With the aim of "touching the world", it uses six languages: English, French, German, Spanish, Arabic and Portuguese. Service is provided to users in all six languages, the same applying to all of FIFA.

---

[13] Extracted from http://www.fifa.com/ (as in February 2012).

com's information and special features. Users can also sign-up to the FIFA.com Club, a service which allows football fans from all over the world to communicate with each other, play games and also comment on the website's articles. Figure 4.15[14] is an example of FIFA website in English.

The two triangulation study's participants (P3.1 and P3.2) were nationals of the same country (Brazil). The experiment was carried out at the Department of Informatics at PUC-Rio, with a duration of approximately two and a half hours. The questionnaire included the same questions as those used in the Case Study (Step Two – Sect. 1.2). We asked about their experience abroad and their knowledge and experience with HCI evaluation. After the researcher presented the experiment goals, the following activities were conducted:

1. The researcher introduced CVM.
2. The participant used CVM to inspect portions of FIFA website in accordance with a compatible scenario.
3. The researcher carried out a post-test interview.

In the scenario we used for this experiment, the participant played the role of someone who had been hired to work in an HCI evaluation of FIFA website. The participant's goal was to evaluate the metacommunication quality (communicability) of the portion about the 2010 FIFA World Cup in South Africa. They should also keep in mind that original designers' intent was, as implied by FIFA's mission statement, to foster the users' contact with cultural diversity within the football domain. However, designers *had not* used CVM to build the website.

Participants also received a cultural information "quick list", with some relevant cultural variables in the football domain: units of measurement, flag colors, language, geography (location, climate, distances and so on), population, fans (preferences, features), how much the World Cup is important for the Host Country, history of football in the Host Country (influences, awards, participation in last World Cups), tourism (accommodation, transportation and so on).

P3.1 and P3.2, then, evaluated the World Cup's portion in Portuguese (see Fig. 4.16[15]) using the following inspection guide:

> A Brazilian fan wants to know everything about South Africa - where and against whom Brazil played, of course. He also wants to learn about this country, to which he hasn't been, yet. Starting from the FIFA's entry page in Portuguese,[16] he selects the FIFA World Cup option. First, he explores the 'Destination' link, with 'Host Cities', 'Stadiums' and 'South Africa A-Z' options. Then, he browses the Teams' section, following the corresponding link.

The experiment procedure was very similar to the one adopted in Step Two, except for some details in the evaluation questionnaire. We used results from Step Two to facilitate the evaluation process (see Sect. 1.2). Our aim was not to solve all

---

[14] http://www.fifa.com/index.html?language=en (as in February 2012).

[15] http://www.pt.fifa.com/worldcup/archive/southafrica2010 (as in February 2012).

[16] http://pt.FIFA.com (as accessed in February 2012).

Fig. 4.15 FIFA website in English (Courtesy of FIFA)

Fig. 4.16   2010 FIFA World Cup South Africa's portion of FIFA website (Courtesy of FIFA)

difficulties with CVM-based evaluation, but only to take the opportunity to improve available scaffolds. This helped us concentrate on more relevant issues for scientific research.

Instead of questions about which cultural variables were used by designers, we asked participants to fill in an evaluation form while they inspected the interface. The form requested the following kinds of information: which web pages (or portions thereof) included traces of cultural variable values (cultural variables in the football domain were listed in the material they had received for the experiment); which interface element(s) was (were) used to express cultural variables and values; and which specific cultural variables were involved in each case.

We also included an additional question at the end of the questionnaire to motivate evaluators in deciding about the global quality of designer-to-user metacommunication. This was the closure question to help them conclude the evaluation, which we found to be missing in Step Two.

4.4.2   Results

We used three categories to analyze discourse material collected during the experiment with FIFA website: difficulties faced during evaluation process; evidence of the epistemic nature of CVM; and evidence that metaphors help designers to inspect and evaluate the communicability of cultural diversity.

4.4.2.1   Difficulties Faced During Evaluation Process

We used this category of analysis to search for problems that required improved explanations and more scaffolds to facilitate a CVM-based evaluation process of cultural aspects of HCI design.

P3.1, for instance, needed a more clearly defined object for evaluation. He said that at first he did not know what to look at in his inspection.

> P3.1: In the beginning I was looking at the interface as a whole, but later on I tried to narrow down on the cultural portion. As far as I see, this cultural portion has more to do with the content than with the interface itself, than with presentation, than with how it is laid out. So, I was more tempted to direct myself to this portion of the [overall] content.

P3.1 also said that although cultural variables helped him through the analysis, he missed some scaffold to support him in identifying the expression of cultural variables in the interface:

> P3.1: Which [interface] elements can characterize the observer at a distance? This is not very clear, but you go on with [your] examination and go on trying to tease them out. Which features, which text, which videos, which images, characterize more [the presence of one] metaphor and less the [presence of] another?

Furthermore, P3.1 had trouble to finish the evaluation and to give his final opinion about the communicability of cultural issues.

> P3.1: How am I to describe this, to say how is it that this fits here, for example, in the 'foreigner with translator' metaphor?

> P3.1: [I found it difficult] to express what I see. How will I indicate [the presence of metaphors] so that whoever is reading my evaluation can understand it? Because I think that if I leave it open [like this], each reader will take the indication in the way he or she wants to. I miss some way to formalize this.

Finally, both participants had trouble to name and indicate website areas where they saw signs (a text or a group of elements) that communicate culture. Here is one piece of evidence:

> P3.2: Perhaps I had difficulty in indicating the location of what I am talking about, isn't it? Because, sometimes, the situation that I saw was something broader, right? It was about the whole section, the whole area. There wasn't a single element in the interface [to point at]. Maybe it was the whole experience. Perhaps I had difficulty there, right? In marking this spot.

4.4.2.2 Evidence of the Epistemic Nature of CVM

Regarding the epistemic nature of CVM, the following sub-categories of meanings were used in this analysis: (i) a mapping of the problem space; (ii) an increased awareness of the designers' own cultural biases and gaps; (iii) a kind of mirror effect, when participants placed themselves in the role of recipients of design communication.

Regarding (i), the mapping of the problem space, CVM guided participants while thinking about the process of communicating culture. P3.1, for instance, said that without CVM he would have thought only about language. CVM helped him to map the problem by comparing cultural variables:

> P3.1: I think that without the metaphors, I would only look at language and, looking at them like this I then tried to see the question with language, cultural practice and the metaphor bit. Without the metaphors I wouldn't have thought of the issues with units of measurement or if the game statistics are shown according to the Brazilian culture or not. I mean, I think that I wouldn't have seen all of this, I would have looked more into the language issue. And also, I wouldn't have thought of the idea of a guided tour visitor: it is there, in South African culture, but more adapted for the Brazilian visitor, in this case.

> P3.1: I think this is very positive because it gives you a guide for what you have to evaluate and also gives you a stand to decide whether the site is more on this side or on that side. If we didn't have that, we wouldn't know, for sure. Because the site behaves as a [bundled] whole.

P3.2 also talked about how the continuum of cultural approximation can help her to understand the problem.

> P3.2: [The continuum is interesting] for you to see… This part of the interface went from where to where? You can see this leap [in the continuum]. Am I always leaping to this place? Do I ever go back? For you to have this perspective on what happened to the traveler on this trip, let's put it like this, I think that this continuum is interesting.

> P3.2: I think it is interesting because you sort of place yourself in that continuum of cultural approximation… because it is a role, isn't it? The role of the traveler. Then you even place yourself in that role and then here am I, lost, needing a hand to pull me up. Then, in another place you say: I am comfortable here, I am at peace here… I think it is even a state, but it is the situation you find yourself in at a given moment.

Regarding (ii), an increased awareness of the designers' own cultural biases and gaps, cultural gaps experienced by participants showed the epistemic potential of CVM in bringing out to the participants aspects of their own knowledge and perceptions regarding other cultures. P3.2, for instance, thought about how to deal with different cultures involved in a cross-cultural application:

> P3.2: In truth, as I am dealing with various countries, in which culture would I be located? Would it be that of the place where the World Cup, the event, took place? Or would it be in the culture? If I were [classified according to] the profile of a [given] country, would it be of that country?

This participant, then, decided to consider that she could think in terms of both her culture (Brazilian) and other cultures:

> P3.2: Because I interpreted it like this: it's my culture and other cultures, independently of whatever they may be [if American, British, African].

For P3.1, because of his own cultural biases and gaps, he felt he should compare FIFA.com with other websites to see whether the interface communicated culture or not:

> P3.1: This other thing, I think it has to do with comparing it with other sites, made for other cultures. Since I was [limited to staying] there, I was sort of not knowing very well if interface elements had to do with culture or not.

Regarding (iii), a kind of mirror effect, we captured the epistemic nature of CVM when P3.2 realized that, by evaluating the website in the light of CVM, she could put herself in the role of the user while trying to understand which strategy was used to communicate culture:

> P3.2: The metaphors are very [closely] associated with the user [stand], with what is his experience or [what we are] trying to make that experience be, you see? Then even in a situation where you want either something deeper or something

shallower for the user's experience, you are always thinking
of that which he goes through while using the website. This
is what I found interesting, because all metaphors are associated with a specific person. So, much depends on the experience
he has, how comfortably or not the user will really go about
having that relation, no matter the level [of immersion] in
other cultures.

The various levels of intercultural contact proposed by CVM also led P3.2 to put
herself in the traveler's role in CVM:

P3.2: To put myself in the shoes of the traveler in the metaphors, to manage to fit there at the moment of interaction, I
think it does help.

P3.2: I was trying, really putting myself in the traveler's
shoes, trying to fit in the options of the continuum, inside
the visitor's graded scale.

As the evidence above suggests, CVM led participants into thinking not only
about the evaluation of FIFA website in itself, but also beyond it, about new ways to
think about cross-cultural systems.

4.4.2.3 Evidence That Metaphors Help Designers to Inspect and Evaluate the Communicability of Cultural Diversity

This category of analysis is based on the following sub-categories of meanings: (i)
a focus on communicability of cultural issues throughout the evaluation process; (ii)
a mapping of the interface; (iii) a naming and framing of the participants' findings
in light of CVM.

With the first sub-category (i), a focus on communicability of cultural issues
throughout the evaluation process, we saw that participants (such as P3.2) realized the
importance of cultural variables for focusing on cultural issues. This is because CVM
operates explicitly on how cultural variables are communicated through interface.

P3.2: This thing about the variables, for instance. You keep
focused on what you are observing.

P3.2: These [metaphor]concepts are really necessary. If I
didn't have these concepts, I wouldn't have had this sort of...
[initiative]: to put myself in the place of the traveler,
within the [spectrum of CVM] metaphors, in order to manage to
fit myself in there at the moment of interaction. I think it
helps indeed.

Like some of the participants in previous experiments, P3.1 and P3.2's happened
to have enough background in Semiotic Engineering, which led them to link the
inspection with CVM with evaluation methods proposed by this theory. P3.2, for
instance, said:

P3.2: I noticed things having to do with communicability here
which, maybe, belong only there, in the Communicability

Evaluation Method. But, when I saw [them], right away, this
level of the domestic traveler and the observer at a distance,
I wondered if the metaphor had any relation with those [com-
municability evaluation] tags which have to do with the location of the person. I kept thinking about that.

With the second sub-category (ii), a mapping of the interface, we found that both
participants realized that sometimes the metaphors were not related to a specific
element or structure, but could be tracked across the whole interactive process. Here
is one piece of evidence.

P3.2: Because, sometimes, the situation that I saw was something broader, right? It was about the whole section, the
whole area. There wasn't a single element in the interface [to
point at]. Maybe it was the whole experience.

P3.1 and P3.2 also had suggestions about how to detect communicability
breakdowns using CVM and communicability evaluation tags [3, 4, 11] to map out
the interface.

P3.1: Some metaphor characteristics have to do with a [com-
municability] tag. It's like CEM [Communicability Evaluation
Method], not that it is the same, but something that already
gives you an idea of, for instance, repetitive things or things
that have similar characteristics. This may constitute a tag
or something like that, something that says that it is a comparison, that it is a text, that it is comparative narrative,
that it is guided tour visitor.

P3.2 proposed that we try to establish a relation between CVM and CEM.

P3.2: I think of it as a complement to CEM, but from a different perspective.

Regarding the third sub-category (iii), a naming and framing of the participants'
findings in light of CVM, P3.2, for instance, was able to name the inspection findings
with CVM concepts:

P3.2: Under the option 'hospitality', if you could classify
it in that continuum, I was at the observer at a distance. I
think that the greatest part of my interaction was in the
observer at a distance. [...] It is the observer at a distance
because this is about culture appearing to the user as information and not as experience. I think this is put forward very
strongly here. It gives me a lot of information. It talks
about what I need, but it doesn't put much experience there.

Furthermore they were able to explain the communicability breakdowns with
CVM. P3.2, for instance, firstly explains the interactive path where she found out
the problem:

P3.2: In the destination section there is the hospitality bit.
I thought he was going to tell me about the people, how the
relations are, if the city is a business center, if it is a
residential area, this area is like this or like that. But,
no! He throws a link that is as if it were more focused on

tourism, you see? He offers me a package telling me how to go
[…] to such and such games. But, I wanted to know what the
people over there are like. But then he sends me … and still
[the] site he sends to me is all in English. And then, I have
a problem there, that he talks about a shopping card, which
he puts it in Euro [values].

P3.2, then, used CVM concepts to explain what happened:

P3.2: So, if this person doesn't know English, then he/she is
left 'without translator'. There he/she was completely lost.
The funny thing is that the link, on the page I am at, in
Portuguese, says 'hospitalidade'. So, I went there, to "hospitalidade", expecting one thing and found something different, in another language. I didn't feel like a foreigner
without translator because I know the language. But had it
been some language that I did not know, I would have really
felt like a foreigner without translator.

P3.2, then, explained how metaphors can help her to find solutions in HCI re-
design. She thought about how to change the intercultural contact level from
observer at a distance to guided tour visitor:

P3.2: So, perhaps he could play a little, even make comparisons between Brazil and South Africa. Perhaps he could even
use his own language, writing in the South African language
and sort of translating it into Portuguese. This way you would
begin to know the language more or less: knowing the language,
knowing the way people speak. Maybe, introducing and blending
these elements and, then, perhaps, it would be more a matter
of experience than simply of information.

P3.2: I think [the contrast] would be a nice feature. Like we
hear it sometimes, right? 'The guy is South Africa's Pelé'.
Trying to make such comparisons: then it all becomes clear.
So, if the guy is the 'South Africa's Pelé' then he is the
best player in the South African team.

In addition to giving evidence of how CVM concepts were interpreted, this category
also showed, as seen above, that participants used them to name their findings and
think further into possible alternatives to communicate the very idea of cultural diversity.

Having arrived at these results with the FIFA experiment we were then able to
conclude this triangulation by identifying the presence or absence of consistent
meanings compared with results identified in the AVIS Case Study. This is what we
present in the final section of this chapter.

4.5 Contrasting Findings from the Studies with AVIS and FIFA Websites

Triangulation reinforced the evidence collected in the case study which suggests
that: CVM have an epistemic effect on the cross-cultural HCI design and evaluation
processes, and CVM help participants in organizing and evaluating communication

about cultural diversity. However, unlike what happened in Step One, participants did not have difficulty in understanding CVM concepts in the FIFA experiment. We believe that this may be the result of improvements we have done in CVM descriptions and examples [12]. Nevertheless, as with participants of Step Two, participants of the triangulation experiment still had trouble to understand what exactly was the object of evaluation and to conclude the evaluation process. Specifically, in both cases some participants were confused or commented that they did not know whether they had to inspect the interface signs in terms of expressions (form) or what they referred to (content). The presence of this sort of evidence suggests that we still have to elaborate concrete examples of what we mean when we talk about communicating culture, in different domains, with special attention to distinguishing between three dimensions in communication: intent, content and expression.

Regarding difficulties to conclude the evaluation process, they sprang from different reasons in experiments with AVIS and FIFA. In the AVIS case study, although participants identified the dominant metaphor, they said that they did not know how to say what was right or wrong because the scenario did not tell them about the specific design intent that designers were trying to achieve. In the FIFA experiment, however, participants faced difficulties in pointing out where exactly there was a piece of communication about culture. This may have been the case for at least two reasons. One is that sometimes there is not, indeed, a specific unitary sign or isolated semiotic structure that communicates culture. This communication may be achieved by an unstructured collection or span of signs appearing along existing interactive paths. The other is that, in the triangulation experiment, participants did not have three re-design alternatives to compare and contrast with each other. The current version of the achieved website on the occasion was the object for evaluation. Consequently, FIFA evaluators did not have alternative designs for comparison, which helps seeing and explaining the benefits of one design alternative over others. For example, a contrastive context helps to see meaning in the *absence* of something in one alternative compared to its *presence* in another.

Regarding epistemic effects, we found consistent evidence that CVM guided participants while their reasoning and judgment about the process of communicating culture in both experiments. All participants valued having CVM concepts and the continuum of cultural approximation available to help them map design and evaluation problems, to learn and think about different levels of intercultural contact through systems interfaces. Moreover, in this process participants got in touch with their own culturally determined assumptions, turning cultural differences into a topic for reflection about themselves, as HCI professionals and researchers.

Lastly, we found consistency among results from all experiments regarding how CVM support HCI practitioners in organizing and evaluating communication about cultural diversity. However, the challenge of focusing on cultural issues apart from other interaction issues throughout the entire evaluation process stood out more clearly only with the FIFA experiment. This is because participants were evaluating an achieved website, and not only partial sketches (which naturally tend to leave out the details that are not directly related to the purpose of the design alternative they represent). This may, in fact, mean that the benefits of CVM in formative and summative evaluation stages of cross-cultural HCI design are not the same. However, further research is obviously needed to explore this possibility, as well as its consequences. Regardless of what may be the case in this respect, however, evidence from the FIFA experiment confirmed that CVM concepts helped participant focus on examining *culture*, as a separable dimension of interaction.

We did not find inconsistency among results obtained with the AVIS and the FIFA studies. Differences in degree of difficulty and variations in perceptions came about precisely because experiments involved different domains (rental cars and football) and different kinds of representation of the design *product* (sketches vs. an achieved artifact). For instance, whereas in Step One we collected evidence that participants thought about how CVM might help them to avoid *introducing* breakdowns in communication. In Step Two they thought about how to detect potential communicative breakdowns in the proposed design (so that they can be corrected in the re-design cycle). In the FIFA Experiment, in turn, they found samples of culture-related communicative breakdowns and they were able to explain them using CVM. Furthermore, in the FIFA experiment, participants suggested that we may create a complementary relationship between CVM and CEM [4, 11] by detecting communicability breakdowns with CVM and using communicability tags to map the interface.

We conclude that the outcome of triangulation was positive, deepening some of the insights we had with previous experiments but never contradicting them. We therefore consider that our research produced valid qualitative results that point at a wealth of further questions for investigation. In next chapter we discuss the value of our approach and present our concluding remarks about the contributions of Semiotic Engineering for dealing with cultural aspects of HCI design.

References

1. Barber, W., & Badre, A. (1998, June 5). Culturability: The merging of culture and usability. In *Proceedings of the 4th conference on human factors & the web*. Basking Ridge: Online publication. Available at http://www.research.att.com/conf/hfweb/proceedings/barber/index.htm. Last visited in Jan 2012.
2. Creswell, J. (2007). *Qualitative inquiry & research design: Choosing among five approaches*. Thousand Oaks: Sage Publications.
3. de Souza, C. S. (2005). *The semiotic engineering of human-computer interaction*. Cambridge: The MIT Press.
4. de Souza, C. S., & Leitão, C. F. (2009). *Semiotic engineering methods for scientific research in HCI*. San Francisco: Morgan and Claypool Publishers.
5. Del Gado, E., & Nielsen, J. (1986). *International user interfaces*. New York: Wiley.
6. Denzin, N., & Lincon, Y. (2008). *The landscape of qualitative research*. Thousand Oaks: Sage Publications.
7. Lazar, J., Dudley-Sponaugle, A., & Greenidge, K.-D. (2004). Improving web accessibility: A study of webmaster perceptions; the compass of human-computer interaction. *Computers in Human Behavior, 20*(2), 269–288.

8. Nicolaci-da-Costa, A., Leitão, C., & Romão-Dias, D. (2001). Gerando conhecimento sobre os homens, mulheres e crianças que usam computadores: algumas contribuições da psicologia clínica. In *Symposium on human factors in computers systems, IHC 2001* (pp. 120–131). Florianópolis: Anais SBC.
9. Nielsen, J. (1994). *Usability engineering*. San Francisco: Morgan Kaufmann Publishers.
10. Nielsen, J., & Mack, R. (Eds.). (1994). *Usability inspection methods*. New York: Wiley.
11. Prates, R. O., de Souza, C. S., & Barbosa, S. D. J. (2000). A method for evaluating the communicability of user interfaces. *ACM Interactions, 7*(1), 31–38.
12. Salgado, L. C. (2011). *Cultural viewpoint metaphors to explore and communicate cultural perspectives in cross-cultural HCI design*. Ph.D. thesis applied to Computer Science Department, PUC-Rio, Brazil. Online at http://www2.dbd.puc-rio.br/pergamum/biblioteca/php/mostrateses.php?open=1&arqtese=0711306_2011_Indice.html. Last visited in February 2012.
13. Schön, D. (1983). *The reflective practitioner: How professionals think in action*. New York: Basic Books.
14. Stephanidis, C., Paramythis, A., Akouminakis, D., & Sfyrakis, M. (1998). Self adapting web-based systems: Towards universal accessibility. In C. Stephanidis & A. Waern (Eds.), *Proceedings of the 4th ERCIM Workshop on 'User Interfaces for All'*, Stockholm, Sweden.
15. Yin, R. (2003). *Case study research: Design and methods*. Thousand Oaks: Sage Publications.

Chapter 5
Final Discussion

Abstract This chapter presents the final discussion of the material presented in this book. We begin with a brief summary of previous chapters, highlighting how the main ideas connected to each other and supported the large structure of argumentation about the value of Cultural Viewpoint Metaphors in the semiotic engineering of cross-cultural interactive discourse. In this summary we emphasize that CVM boost the production of communicative strategies, support the analysis of the overall effects that designers can potentially achieve in metacommunication with users, and help them to identify and isolate cultural dimensions of the interactive discourse. The discussion proceeds with a critical examination of how our proposal relates to selected approaches and theories that have been proposed to address issues that are in some way related to the ones we have addressed. Finally, as closure and conclusion we draw the limits of what we consider our domain of expertise, pointing at areas that our theory cannot reach or has not yet reached. The former represent the scope of opportunities for combining Semiotic Engineering with other approaches and theories, whereas the latter represent the avenues that we plan to follow in future work.

As the Web 2.0 brings about so many opportunities for social interaction and participation online in the second decade of the twenty-first century, systems interface design must deal with culture-determined aspects of the users' experience. Never before has access to foreign culture material – of any kind and in any form – been easier. In fact, for typical Internet users engaged in typical browsing activity, it is rather the exception than the rule to visit only websites that originate from their own culture.

Working with culture, however, is always a challenge. The danger of ethnocentrism is always luring even the noblest aims. Avoiding it is a long-standing concern among social and human scientists. For example, in 1991 Marian Ortuño discussed the importance of cross-cultural awareness in foreign language teaching [18]. Her provocative introduction to her research work is worth quoting:

> Uncontrolled ethnocentrism has often led to prejudice, hatred, oppression, and war. Would it not then be vitally important for educators, especially for those in the field of foreign

L.C.C. Salgado et al., *A Journey Through Cultures: Metaphors for Guiding the Design of Cross-Cultural Interactive Systems*, Human–Computer Interaction Series, DOI 10.1007/978-1-4471-4114-3_5, © Springer-Verlag London 2013

languages and literatures, to instill in their students a sense of cross-cultural awareness by providing them with the tools for identifying their own cultural value orientations as well as those of others? In so doing these students would come away from the typical language course with more than just a minimal exposure to literature and varying degrees of linguistic skill. They would, in addition, be enriched with a global perspective and the ability to recognize the diversity of methods by which different peoples attempt to solve humanity's common problems. [ibid. p. 449]

What Ortuño envisions for foreign language learners can be transposed to the HCI domain. Is it not vitally important, for interaction designers working with systems that intentionally expose their users to foreign culture material, to have a high level of cross-cultural awareness? This book is about *Cultural Viewpoint Metaphors (CVM)*, a Semiotic Engineering tool that – as shown in the long case study reported in Chap. 4 – can help cross-cultural systems designers in "identifying their own cultural value orientations as well as those of others" as a result of thinking about how to communicate with others.

The research presented in this book is a natural unfolding of the particular perspective we hold on human-computer interaction. Our semiotic theory of HCI [6] views human-computer interaction as a specific kind of computer-mediated human communication. In it designers *tell* the users their complete design vision. The designers' message is fully encoded in the system's interface and its interactive patterns. The users receive it and unpack it as they communicate back with the system during interaction. The message speaks of how the designers conceive of the users: the users' needs, knowledge, preferences, expectations, values, goals, activities, location, attitude toward technology and more. It also speaks of how the designers have interpreted the users' problem or envisaged an opportunity that presents itself to them. Their response to this interpretation is precisely the *computer system* that implicitly or explicitly communicates all of this. Most obviously, the designers' message speaks of how the users can or must interact with the system in order to achieve the range goals and effects that the system supports and produces.

The important switch made by Semiotic Engineering, compared to most theories of HCI, is to postulate that designers participate in interaction. Because the designers' message to users is actually a *performative* one (capable of carrying out indefinitely long dialogs with the users) and because what it says is nothing else but what the designers have to communicate, the system interface through which all of this happens actually represents the designers at interaction time. Thus, systems interfaces play more than one role in communication. They are at once a higher-level designer-to-user unfolding *message* and the *sender* and *receiver* of lower-level dialog exchanges with users. This twofold communication process, whose message is itself an interlocutor in lower-level communication processes, characterizes computer-mediated designer-to-user *metacommunication*, Semiotic Engineering's object of investigation.

As it becomes apparent from the above, our perspective on HCI turns designers, just like users, into natives of the *human* side of human-computer interaction. Consequently, subjective dimensions of the designers' profiles and activities can be traced during interaction and can affect the users in different ways [7]. When dealing with cross-cultural systems, the trace of the designers' cultural values as well as their perceptions and interpretations about foreign users' cultural values will, in itself, be the object of users' cultural encounters through metacommunication. For example, while living in North America, one of the authors of this book was the user of a telecommunications company's website that accepted *international credit card* payments for its services. She informed her international credit card number when requested, but *the system* rejected it. She then called the company and spoke to an attendant who plainly repeated what *the system* had said: "international credit cards ARE accepted". The attendant asked the user to go back to the system and inform her credit card number, making sure that she made no mistakes. Once again *the system* rejected it, not surprisingly. The user called the company again and spoke to some manager who eventually realized that *the system* accepted international credit cards *issued by North American banks*.

This incident is a memorable intercultural encounter through technology, especially because it reveals the reach of cultural blunders unconsciously encoded (by designers and developers) in *the systems* that we use anywhere in the world. Ethnocentric interpretations, like what 'international' means when speaking of credit cards, cannot be entirely avoided. All humans perceive and interpret the world from a particular stand point. Therefore, their action and communication is by necessity a sign of this particular positioning. Although there is nothing wrong with it at first step, there begins to be something wrong when we fail to realize that other people do not have the same stand. Nevertheless, it is precisely through minor (or occasionally major) failures of this sort that we *learn* our way out of ethnocentric views and move on to respecting diversity. We cannot learn this by the book. Only personal experience and reflection can teach us the most significant lessons.

The importance of tools mentioned in the quoted passage above (see p. 2) is to leverage the learning process enabled by every single intercultural encounter in human experience. CVM have been conceived to play exactly this role in metacommunication, to leverage the designers' learning about how to communicate with users when different cultural values belong in their message.

We began our research by defining our domain of interest – cross-cultural systems – and object of investigation – culture-sensitive metacommunication. Of course these definitions required further definitions, which we included in this book. We took a very broad perspective on *cross-cultural systems*, defined as those that intentionally expose their users to foreign culture material, and adopted a perspective on *culture* that combined elements of Geertz's interpretive anthropology [9], Hall's intercultural communication approach [10] and finally Danesi and Perron's explorations on the role of signifying orders when analyzing cultures [4]. Together, these concepts helped us to structure our research space by identifying relevant *segmentation* possibilities. At this stage, we work with three of these: (a) classical segmentation between design time and interaction time; (b) segmentation between designer-to-user metacommunication and computer-mediated user-to-user communication; and (c) segmentation of levels of elaboration in the semiotic engineering of designer-to-user metacommunication.

Regarding (a), separating design and interaction contexts when thinking about conceptual tools in HCI is a widely adopted strategy. Although certain tools can be applied in both contexts, results and modes of application are typically different in each case. Therefore, this segmentation is useful to identify distinctions when using CVM in (re)design activities and formative evaluation, as done in Steps One and Two of our Case Study (see Chap. 4, Sects. 4.1 and 4.2), as well as in summative evaluation, as done in the Triangulation Step (see Chap. 4, Sect. 4.3).

Regarding (b), separating designer-to-user metacommunication from computer-mediated user-to-user communication involves more than meets the eye at first glance. Of course there are obvious differences between communication processes in each case (which is why we talk about *metacommunication* in one of them and *computer-mediated communication* in the other). However, there is additional theoretical reason to segment the research space in this way. When users from different cultures communicate with each other through computer systems, they are exposed to the influence of designer-to-user metacommunication. In other words, an adequate analysis of the former should take the latter into consideration. In Chap. 1 (see Sect. 1.3, p. 9), as we were introducing the ideas discussed in this book, we included an illustrative example of how designer-to-user metacommunication can interfere with user-to-user communication in cross-cultural computer-supported collaborative systems. Therefore, this segmentation points at several methodological implications that researchers and practitioners should be aware of when applying CVM to evaluate cross-cultural social systems or to produce and analyze design alternatives for them.

Finally about (c), by segmenting the process of elaborating the designer-to-user interactive discourse to achieve metacommunication through systems interface, we can focus more narrowly on more precisely defined issues and avoid being obfuscated by the presence of others. Our strategy in this particular respect is similar to the one adopted by text generation researchers when they first started to think of computer-generated natural language texts (see, for instance, [11, 13]). Conceptually, they separated text planning from text realization and, within planning, they separated content selection from rhetorical structuring. Transposed to the context of metacommunication design for cross-cultural systems, the segmentation in (c) enabled us to concentrate specifically on the *rhetorical structuring* of metacommunication, that is, on strategies for *organizing* the designers' communication with users at a higher level of abstraction. We did not concentrate on eliciting and selecting intercultural content to be communicated, neither did we concentrate on specifying the final interface design to be implemented in later system development stages. In fact, a large part of the cultural content that designers must communicate can be elicited and selected by means of well-established interaction design methods and tools [19]. Contextual Inquiry [2], Activity Theory [15] and HCI cultural studies conducted with ethnomethodology [8], for instance, can lead to valuable insights in eliciting intercultural content. For the final interface specification, designers must take into consideration many other aspects of HCI besides the ones strictly related to metacommunication. They can resort to a host of existing theories, models, methods and techniques [3] that can complement the semiotic dimensions of metacommunication

Table 5.1 Relations between five conceptual viewpoint metaphors

	Domestic traveler	Observer at a distance	Guided tour visitor	Foreigner with translator	Foreigner without translator
Cultural approximation	0	1	2	3	4
Intensity of mediation	Not applicable	2	3	1	Not applicable

and help them to handle, among others, the cognitive, the ergonomic, the aesthetic and the affective dimensions of interaction design [19].

The result of careful segmentation in our work space locates CVM more clearly in the complex mesh of issues concerning the design of cross-cultural systems. CVM are a conceptual tool that supports designers in producing and evaluating alternative strategies for the organization of intercultural metacommunication. As explained in great detail in Chap. 3, CVM are presented as a set of five structured metaphors where intercultural encounters are viewed as a *journey* and users (the receivers of metacommunication messages) are viewed as *travelers*. The structure of the five metaphors – *the domestic traveler, the observer at a distance, the guided tour visitor, the foreigner with translator* and finally *the foreigner without translator* – correspond to a process of gradual culture approximation, from cultural isolation at one extreme (with *the domestic traveler metaphor*) to complete cultural immersion at the other (with *the foreigner without translator*). The three remaining metaphors require explicit mediation in cultural approximation. Just for sake of simplification (because we explicitly do not consider *measuring* cultural approximation), we can position the five metaphors in relation to each other by using numerical values to represent progression of approximation (from native = 0 to foreign = 4) and intensity of mediation (from low = 1 to high = 3). Table 5.1 expresses how metaphors relate to each other along these two dimensions.

The designers can use Table 5.1 to decide how to position the user in relation to cultural material that is foreign to him or her (this is a decision about cultural approximation). In other words, the designer may organize his communication in such a way that he addresses the user *as* a domestic traveler (i.e. somebody who encounters only material that belongs to his or her native culture), an observer at a distance, a guided tour visitor, a foreigner with translator or a foreigner without translator (i.e. somebody who is on his or her own, totally immersed into a foreign culture environment). Likewise, the designer can use Table 5.1 to decide what level of mediation his communication about cultural diversity will require (i.e. what kinds of scaffolds he will provide to the users so that they will be able and willing to get in touch with material from the foreign culture). The special interest of Table 5.1 is to show that, within the scope of application of any of the five metaphors, decisions about cultural approximation constrain decisions about intensity of mediation and vice-versa.

In the early stages of design or re-design activity, CVM boost the production of communicative strategies and support designers in the analysis and assessment of the overall effects that they can potentially achieve in metacommunication with users. In the final stages of design and development, when high-fidelity prototypes are available, as well as in the evaluation of fully implemented and deployed cross-cultural systems, CVM help HCI professionals to identify and isolate cultural dimensions of empirically observable evidence of interactive discourse.

An extensive case study with CVM was presented in Chap. 4. It involved participants with different cultural backgrounds, engaged in re-design and evaluation tasks proposed in realistic test scenarios with the AVIS website.[1] The results of the case study showed that CVM had a remarkable epistemic effect on the participants, both in design and evaluation contexts. We collected strong evidence that CVM effectively helped participants to formulate deep questions about the users' cultural backgrounds, how they contrasted with foreign culture material communicated in the system, what effects such contrasts might have in successful metacommunication for promoting intercultural contacts through technology, what communicative strategies provide the appropriate support at various degrees of cultural approximation, what levels of cultural mediation support desired degrees of approximation and, last but not least, what signs can be used in interactive discourse in order to awaken the users' interest, understanding and respect for cultural diversity. Just as importantly, and following the inherently reflective character of Semiotic Engineering, participants also gave us strong evidence that CVM helped them to formulate deep questions about *their own* cultural background and positioning in view of the users' culture and all other foreign cultures with which cross-cultural systems design and evaluation requires them to be in contact. This examination of *self* in face of *others* is, we believe, a major first step towards including explicitly, in the design and evaluation of cross cultural systems, some elements of the moral and ethical considerations that Latour proposed to designers in his keynote address to the Design History Society [12]. As was mentioned in Chap. 1 (see Sect. 1.1), Latour is concerned with the designers' ability to identify and somehow express in their designs the *alternative voices*, that is, those that are to greater or lesser extent subdued by the ostensive discourse of winning design choices, those that make their way to the final forms and functions of designed artifacts. Latour's line of thought rests on the undeniable fact that human life has become extensively designed. For example, among the urban population, even health is extensively *designed* in that it is typically the product of carefully selected dosages of food and vitamins, modalities of physical exercise and choice of life style. In view of such depth reached by design activity, those affected by it (i.e. all of us) are morally entitled to know that *there are* alternatives, often very close to the surface of achieved design solutions. Computer artifacts, in this respect, represent a prime opportunity for *voicing* the diversity of values, opinions, expectations and beliefs *of* and *about* their targeted user population.

Cross-cultural systems are among the most sensitive of computer artifacts when it comes to the moral and ethical positioning of their designers, because of the

---

[1] http://www.avis.com/ (as in February 2012).

unavoidable room they make for unconscious (and not so unconscious) ethnocentric attitude and behavior. In this respect, CVM can be used as a tool by designers that mean to understand, respect and protect cultural diversity and to give the users of the products they design the opportunity to do the same. As the case study presented in Chap. 4 also showed, CVM-supported design or evaluation activity has a powerful practical effect: designers and evaluators can isolate cultural issues from other important, but different, human-computer interaction issues. This is an additional *segmentation* compared to the list of segmentations that we have done to delimit the scope of our research (see Chap. 1, Sect. 1.3, p. 9). Here we are talking of segmentation that *HCI practitioners* can do *themselves*, to delimit *their* scope of analysis and focus narrowly on issues that might otherwise get mixed up with other interaction design issues. In fact, one of the participants in the case study explicitly expressed this initial tendency to look at *all* issues bundled together, especially in HCI evaluation tasks. But then, he says, CVM helped to concentrate specifically on cultural issues (see Chap. 4, Sect. 4.2.1, p. 96).

Among the conclusions we draw from the case study is that CVM can transfer to their users (i.e. participants in design and evaluation experiments) a considerable portion of the conceptual and methodological choices that *we* have intentionally made in the process of doing research *about* CVM (but not *with* CVM). For instance, we isolated the cultural dimension from other HCI dimensions (when working *about* CVM). But so did the participants in our experiments (when working *with* CVM). We used elements of the ontology proposed by Semiotic Engineering, Interpretive Anthropology, Intercultural Communication and Cultural Semiotics to name the elements within our research scope, and frame the problem(s) we wanted to investigate (when working *about* CVM). Interestingly, case study participants have also been able to name elements of concern and frame interaction design problems guided by theoretical *meanings* encapsulated into the metaphors and their mutual relations (when working *with* CVM). Finally, we as researchers have reached totally unpredicted conclusions guided by systematic interpretive analysis of our object of investigation (when working *about* CVM), with particular emphasis on how we gained much deeper understanding of insidious ethnocentric biases that must be fought in our own perspective on *culture*. Again the same kind of reflective effect was verified in the participants' experience in cross-cultural systems' re-design and evaluation activities (working *with* CVM). We take this as a powerful demonstration that CVM stimulates what Donald Schön refers to as *reflective practice* [20]. Once again we can hear Latour's call [12] for more attention to ethical considerations in design and say that *reflection in action* and *reflection on action*, to use Schön's well-known terminology, constitute a promising way in that direction.

Although CVM have, as discussed above, observably transferred theory-based knowledge to *their* users (i.e. designers and evaluators who participated in experiments of our case study), improvement is required. In both steps of the case study participants have explicitly manifested technical obstacles in the way CVM have been operationalized. Our aim is that cross-cultural systems' designers and evaluators be able to use CVM without having to be familiar with Semiotic Engineering (as was the case with some of the participants). To this end, we have made adjustments in CVM material that designers and evaluators have used along the case study and the final triangulation experiment. We changed the names of some of the metaphors, revised the definitions of others and worked intensively in the illustrations of use. We also worked on scaffolds, especially for evaluation tasks. For example, we elaborated a questionnaire and form to provide orientation for evaluators that want to examine the organization of intercultural metacommunication discourse in cross-cultural systems. Yet, evidence of difficulties persisted throughout the experiments.

We are fully convinced that we can and should improve CVM technical material. This will certainly facilitate and possibly amplify the transfer of theoretical knowledge *signified* by the concepts, procedures and scaffolds included in technical items. However, it is noteworthy that, as they manifested some of their difficulty and hesitation, participants were often also manifesting powerful new insights and learning. One of the most remarkable instances of this phenomenon was evidenced by one participant who touched on the distinction between *design goal* and *designer's intent*. His comment was:

> P2.3: To answer this question [in the evaluation question-
> naire] I think that there is something missing in terms of
> communication breakdowns. Where does this communication fail
> here? Then, if I had this goal, which one is this metaphor? If
> my goal was to communicate the comparison, why didn't I make the
> comparison correctly? (see Chap. 4, Sect. 4.2.1. p. 98)

Note that he feels that he should know the *design goal* in order to evaluate whether the *designer's intent* to achieve this goal by using a particular metaphor fails or succeeds. Although we can see that the difference between design goal and designer's intent is still unstable in the participant's mind, his attempt at naming the problem that he sees shows the depth of his thoughts about the complexity of designer's task.

If CVM lead HCI practitioners into thinking about their need and ability to trace the *designer's* goal and intent as expressed by interface signs like the rhetorical organization of interactive discourse, then they legitimize and confirm one of the most important theoretical tenets in all semiotic approaches to HCI [1, 5, 14]. Designers, just like users, have goals, intentions, plans and strategies for executing them through systems interfaces. In other words, they are native citizens in the *human* side of HCI. Therefore, when speaking about *human*-computer interaction, we must *also* talk about designers, and not only about users.

This turn has recently been made by one of the founders of User Centered Design (UCD), Don Norman. In one of the most influential books in HCI [16], Norman presented his *Seven Stages of Action* theory, which remained a model for UCD to this date. According to this model, human-computer interaction cycles through seven stages of action, during which users cross two gulfs: the execution and the evaluation [ibid. p. 47] gulfs. Norman was actually talking about acting in the world, and not only of interacting with computers, but for sake of simplicity we present the seven stages in the same way as they have been applied in UCD. The action begins with a *goal*, which leads to an intention to act, then a plan with a sequence of actions, and finally the execution of the action sequence (which triggers the system's response). These stages (except the initial goal) belong to the *execution gulf*, which once bridged by users leads into the traversal of the *evaluation gulf*. There are three more stages in bridging this gulf: perceiving the state of the system, interpreting the perception and evaluating interpretation to decide if the goal has been achieved or if more cycles are needed.

As mentioned previously, the comment made by one of the participants in our case study (somebody who, given his practice in HCI, *knows* UCD and Norman's model) shows that he began to *model the designer's action* using the same conceptual tools as have been used to model the user's action for more than 20 years. The inclusion of designers' goals and actions into a broader model of interaction with contemporary technology, framing use situations as a case of designer-to-user communication, has been done by Norman himself. In his 2011 book [17] he discusses *complexity* and dedicates a full chapter to *social signifiers*, a fundamentally *semiotic* notion, as the author fully acknowledges. But, perhaps more important to make our point in this discussion, Norman's new semiotic perspective – motivated by his thoughts on how we live with complex systems – is tightly coupled with the role of communication in design. Here is what he says:

> The major path to good, usable design is communication. Once upon a time the word 'design' referred primarily to appearances: automobile styling, fashions, and interiors. Products were viewed in photographs, prizes awarded solely on the basis of appearance. Today that has changed: the design world now is concerned with function and operation, with fulfilling fundamental needs, with delivering positive, enjoyable experiences. We now recognize that one critical component of good design is good interaction, and interaction, to a large extent, is about proper communication. [ibid. p. 225]

We thus come to the conclusion of this book in which we want to underline something that has in fact been one of the leitmotifs in preceding chapters as well as in this one: *segmentation*. All theories *segment* the world in particular ways. By so doing, they allow us to isolate specific phenomena of interest and to inspect them in detail without being distracted by other phenomena in which we are not interested at that particular moment. One of the pitfalls in research is to become so captivated by one theory that we forget that *there is more* outside the segment we can see with it. Could we metaphorically refer to this risky situation as *scientific ethnocentrism*?

The question is on the verge of rhetoric. This book is about culture-sensitive discourse in technology, based on a semiotic theory of HCI which, as shown mainly in Chaps. 1 and 2, achieves a profoundly reflective effect. In the semiotic engineering of human-computer interaction, an extensive part of what designers are doing is to build their deputy at design time, namely their representation of *self*. Therefore, we have good reason to assume that HCI design is laden with culture-sensitive material even if the system being designed is not a cross-cultural system as defined in this volume. All human beings engaged in social interaction of any sort wear their cultural origins on their sleeves.

This perspective is a contribution of CVM to Semiotic Engineering itself, which up to now did not have the right concepts to name and frame issues of cultural determination in metacommunication as a clearly defined object of investigation. However, going back to segmentation and trying to avoid the kind of scientific ethnocentrism we introduced above, we see that Semiotic Engineering is (as all others) a partial theory of HCI. In other words, it can only account for a *segment* of the whole complexity involved in this fascinating phenomenon: the communication of designers to users, which unfolds as users communicate with the system. Even more precisely, Semiotic Engineering is interested in *communicating* the designers' message and in analyzing how it is received by users. One of the important segments *left out* of this picture, among many others, is how we discover what there is to be communicated in the first place.

Our study of anthropological theories of culture in the course of this research has reinforce our belief that Semiotic Engineering can be very productively combined with ethnomethodology and improved our understanding of why this is the case. In a previous book about Semiotic Engineering methods for scientific research in HCI [7] we had already suggested that Contextual Inquiry [2] and Activity Theory [15] could be used in conjunction with our theory to cover fundamentally important steps at the beginning of the interaction design cycle. However, as the ideas presented in this book have shown, we have to deal with cultural aspects of HCI even in domains that don't seem to have anything to do with culture. Think of the international credit card anecdote reported at the beginning of this chapter. Could anyone guess that online commercial transactions provided by some North American company to clients living in North America would lead into cultural blunders? Most probably not. The new question is: would an ethnomethodological approach to studying and modeling this system's domain miss it? Actually, this is not a new question at all. In the late 1980s Lucy Suchman, for instance, had already warned the HCI community about this [21].

In the near future, we will be working on the technical enhancement of CVM scaffolds in order to improve this epistemic tool's *usability*. On the theoretical front we will keep exploring the implications of this work for Semiotic Engineering and for HCI, constantly looking for the meta-theoretical meanings that we occasionally discover as we tread this path.

References

1. Andersen, P. B. (1997). *A theory of computer semiotics: Semiotic approaches to construction and assessment of computer systems* (2nd ed.). Cambridge: Cambridge University Press.
2. Beyer, H., & Holtzblatt, K. (1998). *Contextual design: Defining customer-centered systems.* San Francisco: Morgan Kaufmann.
3. Carroll, J. M. (2003). *HCI models, theories and frameworks: Toward a multidisciplinary science.* San Francisco: Morgan Kaufmann Publishers.
4. Danesi, M., & Perron, P. (1999). *Analyzing cultures: An introduction and handbook.* Bloomington: Indiana University Press.
5. de Souza, C. S. (2005). Semiotic engineering: Bringing designers and users together at interaction time. *Interacting with Computers,* Elsevier, *17*(3), 317–341.
6. de Souza, C. S. (2005). *The semiotic engineering of human-computer interaction.* Cambridge: The MIT Press.
7. de Souza, C. S., & Leitão, C. F. (2009). *Semiotic engineering methods for scientific research in HCI.* San Francisco: Morgan and Claypool Publishers.

8. Dourish, P., & Bell, G. (2011). *Divining a digital future mess and mythology in ubiquitous computing*. Cambridge: MIT Press. http://site.ebrary.com/id/10476094.
9. Geertz, C. (1973). *The interpretation of cultures: Selected essays*. New York: Basic Books.
10. Hall, E. T. (1976). *Beyond culture*. New York: Doubleday.
11. Hovy, E. H. (1988). *Generating natural language under pragmatic constraints*. Hillsdale: Lawrence Erlbaum Associates.
12. Latour, B. (2009). A cautious prometheus? A few steps toward a philosophy of design (with special attention to Peter Sloterdijk). In Fiona Hackne, Jonathn Glynne and Viv Minto (editors) Proceedings of the 2008 Annual International Conference of the Design History Society. Falmouth, 3–6 September 2009, e-books, Universal Publishers, pp. 2–10.
13. McKeown, K. R. (1985). *Text generation: Using discourse strategies and focus constraints to generate natural language text*. Cambridge: Cambridge University Press.
14. Nadin, M. (1988). Interface design and evaluation: Semiotic implications. In H. R. Hartson & D. Hix (Eds.), *Advances in human-computer interaction 2* (pp. 45–100). Norwood: Ablex.
15. Nardi, B. A. (1996). *Context and consciousness: Activity theory and human-computer interaction*. Cambridge: MIT Press.
16. Norman, D. A. (1988). *The design of everyday things*. New York: Doubleday.
17. Norman, D. A. (2011). *Living with complexity*. Cambridge: MIT Press.
18. Ortuño, M. M. (1991). Cross-cultural awareness in the foreign language class: The Kluckhohn model. *The Modern Language Journal, 75*, 449–459.
19. Rogers, Y., Sharp, H., & Preece, J. (2011). *Interaction design: Beyond human-computer interaction* (3rd ed.). Chichester: Wiley.
20. Schön, D. (1983). *The reflective practitioner: How professionals think in action*. New York: Basic Books.
21. Suchman, L. (1987). *Plans and situated actions: The problem of human-machine communication*. New York: Cambridge University Press.

Index

C

Communicability, 91, 96, 98, 100, 103, 106, 107, 109, 110, 113
Communication
    computer-mediated, 15, 16, 20, 30, 37, 118
    definition of, 23
    intercultural, 9, 10, 14, 33–35, 37, 39, 117, 121
Cross-cultural systems
    definition of, 1, 8, 12, 15, 117
    ethical considerations on, 16, 120, 121
    semiotic engineering of, 12, 16, 38, 116, 117, 121
Culturability, 96
Cultural
    accessibility, 2, 6
    differences, 12, 30, 35, 39, 44, 47, 74, 80, 90, 112
    dimensions, 30, 31, 113, 115, 120, 121
    markers, 49, 52, 57, 58, 60, 65
    mediation, 13, 44, 45, 49, 54, 57, 120
    variables, 15, 33, 37, 39, 45–50, 54, 60, 65, 71, 87, 91, 100, 103, 106
Cultural diversity, 1, 2, 10, 12, 15, 16, 31, 36–40, 43, 44, 47, 56, 74, 77, 80, 87, 89–91, 94, 95, 98, 100, 103, 106, 109–112, 119–121
Cultural viewpoint metaphors
    contribution to HCI research, 69
    contribution to semiotic engineering, 116, 123
    definition of, 1, 2, 12, 40, 43, 44, 116, 119
    domestic traveler, 12, 13, 44, 47, 48, 75, 76, 119

    epistemic value of, 46, 76, 79, 87, 93, 100, 106–108, 111, 112, 115, 120
    foreigner without translator, 13, 44, 60, 61, 63, 64, 66, 119
    foreigner with translator, 13, 44, 56–58, 60, 66, 74, 75, 81, 88, 99, 119
    guided tour visitor, 13, 15, 44, 52, 54, 56, 66, 74, 75, 81–83, 88, 119
    observer at a distance, 13, 48, 50, 52, 66, 74, 75, 83, 119
Culture
    definitions of, 9, 10, 30, 32–36
    Eco's perspective on, 30, 32, 35
    ethnography, 15, 31–33, 74
    ethnomethodology, 39, 118, 124
    Geertz's perspective on, 9, 10, 32–35, 39, 40, 117
    Hall's perspective on, 10, 33–35, 39, 117
    HCI research on, 10, 19, 33, 37
    Hofstede's perspective on, 9, 10, 35
    the role of culture in Semiotics, 30, 33
Culture-sensitive interaction, 1, 2, 19, 33, 35–37

D

Designer's deputy, 7, 8, 20, 22, 23, 26, 29, 39, 43–45
Domestic traveler, 12, 13, 44, 47, 48, 75, 76, 119

F

Foreigner without translator, 13, 44, 60, 61, 63, 64, 66, 119
Foreigner with translator, 13, 44, 56–58, 60, 66, 74, 75, 81, 88, 99, 119

G
Guided tour visitor, 13, 15, 44, 52, 54, 56, 66, 74, 75, 81–83, 88, 119

H
Human-Computer Interaction (HCI) design
    activity theory, 24, 33, 118, 124
    ethnomethodology, 39, 118, 124
    Latour perspective, 2–4, 8, 16, 21, 120, 121
    participatory design, 10, 37
    usability, 3, 4, 86, 96, 124
    user centered design, 3, 6, 122
Human-Computer Interaction (HCI)
        evaluation, 70, 87, 89, 96, 101, 103, 121

I
Intercultural encounters, 1, 37–39, 117, 119
Internationalization, 12, 45
Internationalization-localization, 10, 43

L
Localization, 10

M
Meanings, 3–6, 9, 10, 12, 15, 23, 24, 26–28, 30, 31, 33, 36, 39, 40, 44, 71, 74, 76, 121, 124

Metacommunication
    definition of, 4, 15, 16
    in human-computer interaction, 7
    message, 7, 11, 12, 20, 21, 25, 26, 35, 47, 66, 119
    strategy, 12, 16, 45, 81–83, 108, 118

O
Observer at a distance, 13, 48, 50, 52, 66, 74, 75, 83, 119

S
Semiotic engineering
    definition of, 4, 15, 20, 116
    ontology, 22–24, 38
    tools (MAC, SIM, Molic), 26, 43
    unit of investigation, 6–8, 20–22, 24, 116, 124
Semiotics
    cultural, 10, 31, 36, 117, 121
    definition of, 4
    Eco's semiotics, 19, 23, 30
    Peirce's semiotics, 19, 23
Signification, 23
Signification systems, 12, 23, 24, 29, 30, 34, 35, 39, 40, 44
Signs
    dynamic, 5, 6, 15, 26–29
    metalinguistic, 5, 6, 15, 26, 28, 29, 35
    Peirce's definition, 23
    static, 5, 6, 15, 26–29